# Faith for
# the Journey

Books in this series . . .

# A BIBLE STUDY ON HEBREWS

# *Faith for the Journey*

## REUBEN R. WELCH

FRANCIS ASBURY PRESS
of Zondervan Publishing House
Grand Rapids, Michigan

FRANCIS ASBURY PRESS is an imprint of Zondervan Publishing House
1415 Lake Drive, S.E., Grand Rapids, Michigan 49506

**Library of Congress Cataloging in Publication Data**

Welch, Reuben.
    Faith for the journey : a Bible study on Hebrews.

    1. Bible. N.T. Hebrews—Criticism, interpretation, etc. I. Title.
BS2775.2.W45    1988        227'.8707      88-192424
ISBN 0-310-75311-2

Designed by Ann Cherryman

*Printed in the United States of America*

88  89  90  91  92  93  94  95 / CH / 10  9  8  7  6  5  4  3  2  1

# CONTENTS

# Preface

● The letter to the Hebrews is different from other New Testament letters. The others usually begin with the identification of the writer and the readers, followed by a greeting and a thanksgiving. A good example is Philippians 1:1–2: "Paul and Timothy, servants of Christ, To all the saints in Christ Jesus who are at Philippi, with the bishops and deacons: Grace to you and peace from God our Father and the Lord Jesus Christ." All of Paul's letters begin this way, as do those of Peter, James, and Jude. Hebrews begins with a declaration that God has spoken supremely and sovereignly through his Son in these last times.

There is no indication of authorship in Hebrews. Nothing is said about who or where the readers are. Hebrews closes, however, much like a letter and even mentions Timothy, "our brother," who recently "has been released" (13:23). There are those who wonder if it is a letter at all. The writer himself calls it "my word of exhortation" (13:22), as though it were a written sermon, designed to be read to the congregation.

One of the fascinating things about Hebrews is that it brings up all kinds of questions that cannot be specifically answered. Who is the author? Who are the readers? When was it written and why?

Several considerations have led most evangelical scholars to the conclusion that, though possible, it is highly improbable that Paul was the author of Hebrews. For one thing, Paul's name is not mentioned in any of the oldest manuscripts. The added titles only say "To the Hebrews." For another, the language and style of Hebrews is different from any of Paul's letters. Hebrews uses high-class, literary Greek; Paul's style is impulsive, personal, and

7

broken. Then also, Paul, the Pharisee, was concerned with the law. In fact, Christ had freed him from the bondage to the law as the means of producing righteousness. Hebrews, however, is at home in the rituals and sacrifices of the priestly system in Israel. Christ is portrayed as our high priest who, as our sacrifice for sin, mediates a better covenant, bringing us into the presence of God.

If there is general agreement that Paul did not write Hebrews, there is certainly no agreement as to who else might have—there are only guesses. One commentator has suggested that the author of Hebrews remains "tantalyzingly anonymous." A strange name, to be sure. We could, perhaps, just call him "T. A." for short. We do know that "Anonymous" has been credited with an amazing amount of literature!

The position taken in this study is that Hebrews was written from Rome to a church in which a group of Jewish Christians were in danger of losing heart and hope and rejecting God's final revelation in Christ; written probably a few years before the destruction of the temple in Jerusalem in A.D. 70.

For all the questions this magnificent book raises, there is no question as to its profound understanding of the gospel, its marvelous exaltation of Christ, and its amazing ability to exhort and warn us in the context of our own culture. Through Hebrews we are challenged to follow Christ, our priestly leader, who "endured as seeing him who is invisible" (11:27) and calls us to follow.

# CHAPTER · 1

# Do We Really Believe the Gospel?

In many and various ways God spoke of old to our fathers by the prophets; but in these last days he has spoken to us by a Son, whom he appointed the heir of all things, through whom also he created the world. He reflects the glory of God and bears the very stamp of his nature, upholding the universe by his word of power. When he had made purification for sins, he sat down at the right hand of the Majesty on high. . . .

Therefore we must pay the closer attention to what we have heard, lest we drift away from it. For if the message declared by angels was valid and every transgression or disobedience received a just retribution, how shall we escape if we neglect such a great salvation? . . .

Take care, brethren, lest there be in any of you an evil, unbelieving heart, leading you to fall away from the living God (Heb. 1:1–3; 2:1–3; 3:12).

● What a fascinating book Hebrews is! Not easy, but fascinating, and if we will listen, it is life transforming. We know surprisingly little about it. No one knows for sure to whom it was written, but I am convinced that it was written to us. It comes right out of the Old Testament and speaks of ancient covenant symbols, yet it comes right into our world and speaks to us of new covenant realities. It is filled with ancient Hebrew ritual, yet it finds and meets the real needs of contemporary Gentiles.

## ● A Great Heritage

The little that is known about the first readers of this book only emphasizes how much like them we are and how much we need their message. For example, they shared a wonderful heritage. They were in a long line of priests and prophets, judges and kings. In their history were temple and ritual, altar and sacrifice. They were the proud possessors of law and nationhood. They remembered great leadership and great deliverance; their very existence was the result of great divine providence.

Moreover, their wonderful heritage had been brought to fulfillment in the complete salvation accomplished by the very Son of God. They had experienced the powers of the new age which his coming had inaugurated. They shared the gift of his life and knew the living presence of the Holy Spirit. Those first readers were a privileged people.

They were also people with tremendous needs. Passing time and eroding pressures had dulled their joy, distracted their vision, and weakened their loyalties. They had forgotten who they were and what they had received. They needed new vision, new perspective, and a new commitment.

We can identify with these early Christians who first listened to the words of Hebrews. We, too, have a great heritage, but like them, we have allowed the pressures and struggles of life to overturn our priorities and drain our vitality. We have forgotten who we are and desperately need to recover our true identity and our meaning.

## ● Great Theology

The writer's response to their needs—and ours—is this written sermon of thirteen chapters, which he calls his "word of exhortation" (13:22). In this word he undergirds them with great theology. He speaks of God, the sovereign creator God who partially and diversely revealed himself in other times and has now in these last days made himself known in his Son, Jesus Christ. This Son, who is sovereign, became incarnate, died a sacrificial death, and opened the way to God. He ministers to our deepest needs by a continuing intercession on our behalf as our high priest.

No book in the New Testament exalts so highly the true divinity of Christ, the Son of God. Yet no New Testament book speaks more frankly, more candidly of his genuine humanity. He cried great groanings and endured great suffering; he became the pioneer and perfecter of our faith.

The Hebrews knew these things about Jesus. So do we. Yet they were in danger of drifting and forgetting and losing the most precious reality of their lives. The question posed by the book is, do we really believe what God has done in Jesus? We know the great theme of theology: the sovereign, creator, Father God entered into the stream of our world's history in Jesus Christ our Lord. We claim to know this truth. *Do we, really?* Are we fully convinced of the finality of Jesus Christ? Are we totally committed to the uniqueness of Jesus Christ and the supremacy of his gospel? More directly, have we, in the depths of our souls, with all of life on the line, committed ourselves to the revelation of God in Jesus Christ?

There are other views, other voices, competing for our loyalty. I think, for instance, of the world of science and technology. Scientific research opens up vast areas of knowledge; technology increasingly brings discoveries within our reach and usefulness. In the process they exercise increasing control over our lives. Every new technology is used by the entertainment industry to stimulate our fantasies, our imaginations, and our emotions. A world view, a perception of reality, is created by movies, television, videos, tapes, and records. New discoveries and technologies make possible incredible developments in the world of medicine. Vast knowledge has increased our ability to change, control, and manipulate our physical bodies. Our understanding of ourselves and our world is profoundly affected by such developments as contraception, artificial insemination, surrogate parenting, organ transplants, and genetic engineering. Our massive scientific developments have opened up space and created weaponry capable of annihilating the human race that created it.

The point is that the human exploitation of scientific knowledge and technology presupposes a world without God, without intrinsic value and without ultimate purpose. We are in control. What we can do, we will do without restraint. Who we are as a human species and what we are to become are questions that we ourselves deign to answer. This perspective has tremendous appeal. It speaks with a powerful voice to the secular mind.

The scientific-technological explosion has alongside it a growing pluralism of value systems. Christianity is no longer the dominant and controlling influence on values, lifestyles, and beliefs. Everyone must agree in school that two plus two equals four. That is fact, and no disagreement is acceptable. However, the idea that morality is better than immorality or that greed is destructive or that God has revealed himself in Jesus—these are not agreed; they are made relative to whatever background, training, or opinion one may have. So monogamy, promiscuity, or homosexuality may each be right for the person who makes the decision. Christianity, Buddhism, Islam, Science of Mind, and Satan worship are all open and presumably acceptable alternatives as religious beliefs.

Amid these other perspectives, other religions, other points of view, other voices calling for attention, the question posed by the book of Hebrews could not be more important for us. Do we really believe the gospel? Is Jesus Christ, God's Son, our brother, redeemer, high priest, and Lord? The presence of other loud and assertive voices makes our response all the more urgent and all the more significant. We cannot drift with the borrowed values and priorities of an assumed Christian culture—we must choose. Our meaning, our purpose as humans, our place in the earth—these cannot be presumed to be accepted and secure. They are at terrible risk. What are we going to do with the claims of Christ?

Those to whom Hebrews was written were also hearing other voices and perceiving other options. The writer does not attack the other options as much as he proclaims vital theology. He confronts his readers with the great reality of the creator, redeemer God who has come in Jesus Christ his Son. Our meaning, our purpose, and our hope are in him. He is the incarnate one who discloses the meaning of reality, he is the final revelation of God and the high priest of our salvation. He, then, is the center of life for us who believe the gospel.

God's deed in Christ is the supreme redemptive reality for everyone and not just those who happen to have been brought up in church. His redemption is complete for everyone and not just those obsessed with personal guilt. He is the key to ultimate reality; that means for all mankind and not just those who reject the secularism of science and technology. The book of Hebrews will not concede that Christianity is one option among many. It will not agree that Christ is one revelation among many or that his death is one sacrifice among many. We are called to respond to the finality of Jesus Christ, to believe the gospel and join the community of faith, the pilgrim people of God.

## ● Great Exhortations

In Hebrews is also found great exhortation. In fact, the book is made up of alternating declarations and exhortations.

— Since God has spoken by his Son who is higher than the angels, "we must pay the closer attention to what we have heard, lest we drift away from it" (2:1).

— Since Christ is faithful over God's house, not as a servant like Moses, but as a Son, we should take care and avoid the "evil and unbelieving heart" (3:12).

— Since the promise of a sabbath rest remains for the people of God, "let us therefore strive to enter that rest, that no one fall by the same sort of disobedience" that trapped the children of Israel in the wilderness (4:11).

— "Since we have a great high priest who has passed through the heavens, Jesus, the Son of God, let us hold fast our confession" (4:14).

— Since Christ is a high priest after the order of Melchizedek, let us not become "dull of hearing," but "leave the elementary doctrine of Christ and go on to maturity" (5:8–6:1).

— "Therefore, brethren, since we have confidence to enter the sanctuary by the blood of Jesus, . . . let us hold fast the confession of our hope without wavering" (10:19, 23).

— Since we are surrounded with such a great cloud of witnesses, "let us lay aside every weight, and sin which clings so closely and let us run with perseverance the race that is set before us" (12:1).

The writer to the Hebrews knew that great theology is never enough. The proclamation of Christ calls for attention. The things we have heard call us to follow. We who share a heavenly call are exhorted to be concerned about our heart response, our trustful openness to our high priest. We need to share the rest of God, who rested from his creative labors on the Sabbath. We are exhorted to cease from our labors in obedient trust and rest. A thousand voices call, a thousand doubts plague us; therefore we are exhorted to hold fast our confidence all the way through. We are not to give up our faith and our hope and our confession of Christ.

The alternative to drifting is growth and advancement. The path ahead is open-ended, and we are called to grow up and mature and learn to endure the hardships of the journey. Christ has accomplished a real atonement for sin and has opened the way to God. We are urged to draw near in confidence and assurance that we are loved and he is faithful. The Old Testament heroes of faith and, finally, Jesus, our New Covenant leader, call us to run the race of the Christian life. Our sights are to be fixed on Jesus himself who suffered, endured, and triumphed.

These are some of the exhortations given to the Hebrews. To read them is to know that they are for all of us. Our needs are surprisingly like theirs. We need to hold on in spite of disillusionment and discouragement, in spite of pain and loss. We need to remember that we are a servant-pilgrim people of the one who had no place to lay his head. Do we know how to be followers of the one who endured through suffering and died on a hill outside the city gates?

We need the exhortations to remind us of our forefathers and forerunners in the faith who "suffered mocking and scourging, and even chains and imprisonment. They were stoned, they were sawn in two, they were killed with the sword; they went about in skins of sheep and goats, destitute, afflicted, ill-treated—of whom the world was not worthy—wandering over deserts and mountains, and in dens and caves of the earth" (11:36–38). These are our people. Have we forgotten our lineage and our heritage?

We need to get a new grip on the reality of God, the sovereignty of Christ, the total sufficiency of his atoning death, and the sustaining strength of his continuing priesthood. These are not just pious words. They express the real needs of our hearts in our real world.

How many have lost will and lost hope because they trusted their own strength and character and were disillusioned by the "plague of their own hearts"? Where is hope, where is confidence for the future, where is energy and vitality for ministry? It is not in ourselves or in the closed systems of political power. It is only in our trustful, obedient response to God's redemptive deed in Christ. "Lord, to whom shall we go? You have the words of eternal life" (John 6:68). The exhortations, then, do not say to us, "Try harder, be stronger, grit your teeth and endure." They say, rather, "Remember who you are! Listen, pay attention, hang on to your confidence and trust, keep the faith!"

## • Great Warnings

The book of Hebrews is also a book of great warnings. Along with the assurance of divine provision are hard, almost shocking descriptions of the consequences of disobedience and rejection. We will talk of some later, but it is very clear that the Hebrews were in danger. Continued faith and hope in the gospel are not matters of indifference. The prevailing attitude in our pluralistic culture today is that choices of values and lifestyles are matters of private and not public concern. Each person has the right to choose the morals and priorities that seem best suited to the situation.

Years ago I read that the first century A.D. was a time when all religions were regarded by the general population as equally true, by the philosophers as equally false, and by the politicians as equally useful. Our own century is little changed in attitude. It was not an easy thing for the Hebrews to reject all other options and put their whole lives in Jesus Christ alone. But this is precisely what was called for.

The call was intensified by a series of warnings that placed before the Hebrews the moral significance of their choices—and their un-choices. They were warned against neglecting the great salvation God had provided through Christ; they were in danger of drifting away from the saving message. Through their hardness of heart they could fall short of the goal of God's promised rest for them; worse, they could fall away from the living God. They were in danger of the dullness of hearing and the deliberate sinning that would lead to apostasy, with its fearful prospect of judgment. They were losing confidence, giving place in their hearts to the bitterness that could lead them to a refusal of the God who speaks the word of judgment and of salvation.

What warnings are here for us? We need to know that obedience to the gospel or rejection of it is a moral choice with eternal consequences. Great gain and great loss are at stake. A casual approach to God's deed in Christ is frightening. I am not thinking of those who have never heard—I am thinking of us who, like the Hebrews, have heard the Word, who have tasted the heavenly gift, who are partakers of the Holy Spirit, who are the "enlightened" ones who know the truth (6:4–5). I am thinking about us of whom it could be said that we still need to be taught when we should be teachers, that we should be on solid food and are still on pabulum. Can we know that the issues are ultimate and urgent? Can we ever understand that drift is deadly and hard-heartedness is costly and disobedience is damning?

I wonder if underneath our careless attitude toward the gospel is a fundamental doubt about the finality of Jesus Christ. Could it be that behind our superficial commitment and our compromised morals is the thought that the gospel doesn't really matter all that much? Is it hard for us to accept the gospel's radical demands because we don't really believe it?

## ● Conclusion

In the book of Hebrews there is great theology. It is focused in God's final self-revelation in Jesus Christ, his Son, who accomplishes our redemption through his own self-giving in death and who is our continuing high priest.

There is great exhortation to respond to the salvation of God through Christ with continuing faith and loyalty. These exhortations are combined with warnings against falling back, losing confidence, giving up and finally forsaking the faith.

The book reveals profound understanding of the gospel, deep pastoral concern for its readers, and a clear sense of urgency about the acceptance of the message. The book also asks profound questions of us who read it: Do we really believe the gospel? Will we receive for ourselves the exhortations to be strong in the Lord, to grow up in him, to hang on and endure? Will we heed the warnings?

Life's ultimate issues are on the line, issues of life or death, heaven or hell. Everything is to gain and everything is to lose. Therefore, "let us also lay aside every weight, and sin which clings so closely, and let us run with perseverance the race that is set before us, looking to Jesus the pioneer and the perfecter of our faith, who for the joy that was set before him endured the cross, despising the shame, and is seated at the right hand of the throne of God" (12:1–2).

## ● Discussion Questions

1. It is very important to know as much as we can about the Hebrews who received this letter. Before we begin to study the book we need to read it through. As you read, what do you discover about their situation and the threats to their faith and fellowship?

2. In what ways do you see the needs of the Hebrews to be similar to our own?

3. The writer undergirds all he says with the great declaration that God has revealed himself in Jesus Christ. What makes this declaration so significant? In what other ways has God revealed himself? What would we know about God if he had not come in Jesus?

4. From your reading in Hebrews, what is faith? Is it any different for the writer of Hebrews than for Paul in the book of Galatians or the book of Romans? Explain your answer.

5. I have talked about the world of science and technology as offering an alternative world view to that of the Christian world view expressed in the Bible. What other alternative views can you think of? What does Hebrews teach us about how to respond to such views?

6. Why are some of the warnings in Hebrews so severe? How can warnings be given without communicating the idea that the gospel is drudgery and effort, based on fear of being lost?

7. According to Hebrews, there is a difference between "believing the gospel" and "*really* believing the gospel." What is that difference?

# C H A P T E R · 2

# God Has Spoken in His Son

In many and various ways God spoke of old to our fathers by the prophets; but in these last days he has spoken to us by a Son, whom he appointed the heir of all things, through whom also he created the world. He reflects the glory of God and bears the very stamp of his nature, upholding the universe by his word of power. When he had made purification for sins, he sat down at the right hand of the Majesty on high, having become as much superior to angels as the name he has obtained is more excellent than theirs (Heb. 1:1–4).

● At the heart of the theology of Hebrews is God's revelation of himself in Jesus. The writer knew all about Israelite history and worship, but somewhere along his journey he met Christ—and all the partial and fragmentary pieces of salvation history came together. From that time, like Paul, the writer determined to know nothing but Christ. His whole horizon was filled with his grandeur and his wonder.

In the brief, magnificent paragraph of Hebrews 1:1–4, the writer witnesses to the finality of the supreme revelation of God in Christ as compared with the partial and preparatory revelation under the old covenant. All the ways that God had made himself known to his creatures through the centuries came to fulfillment in the word spoken through the life and death of Jesus. The center of all revelation is Christ, who reflects the Father's nature, mediates the Father's creation, and accomplishes the Father's redemption.

## • We Know God Through the Son

The Hebrews came to know God as their creator because they first knew him as their redeemer. In the experience of the Exodus, God delivered his people from bondage. Through that crucial event they understood themselves to be the people of God's choosing. They experienced redemption and then understood that their redeemer was also their creator, the maker of heaven and earth.

In the same way we know God as our creator because we first know him as our redeemer in Jesus Christ our Lord. It is not that we first know God, then come to know his Son. We know God only because we first know the Son through whom the Father has revealed himself. What we understand about God we understand only because he has spoken in his Son.

The wonder is that God has spoken. He is not a god who has closed himself and withheld himself from us. He has taken the initiative and has opened himself to his creatures. He spoke first in creation—"By the word of the Lord the heavens were made" (Ps. 33:6)—and in the creation narrative. "God said—and it was so" (Gen. 1:9).

Beginning with his call to his fallen creatures in Eden, "Adam, where are you?" God has spoken to his people and revealed himself through the events of their history. In many ways and in many forms God communicated with his people, now one way, now another; now one truth, now another. To the patriarchs and Moses, the judges and the kings, through the Exile and the return, God revealed himself. Through the ordinances, the declarations, the symbolic actions of sacrifices and offerings, the rituals of worship; through the law of the priests, the word of the prophets and the wisdom of the sages, the character and the purposes of God were gradually and variously disclosed.

Yet none of these fully expressed what God wanted to say. Then, "when the time had fully come, God sent forth his Son" (Gal. 4:4). His final word was uttered when Jesus came. The "Word" who was with God and was God "became flesh and dwelt among us" (John 1:14). "In many and various ways God spoke of old to our fathers by the prophets; but in these last days he has spoken to us by a Son" (Heb. 1:1). All the forms of God's previous self-revelation are now fulfilled and transcended in the final word, the word made flesh. "All the promises of God find their Yes in him. That is why we utter the Amen through him" (2 Cor. 1:20).

The prophet cried, "Hear, O heavens, and give ear, O earth; for the Lord has spoken" (Isa. 1:2). The Preacher declares, "God . . . has spoken to us by a Son." The whole Bible tells us that God speaks. The question is, "What does he say?" The answer is clear and profoundly significant: God says Jesus. Jesus is the lived-out word of the creator-revealer-redeemer God. The word that is the extension of God, that expresses the person of God, is not a voiced declaration, not a written proclamation, but a person. The Father speaks the word—the word that conveys his character and his will—by the breath of his Spirit: the Father, the Breath, and the Word. That word became flesh in Jesus Christ our Lord, the personal, lived-out word of God, breathed by the Spirit, spoken by the Father, displaying before our human eyes his nature and his purpose.

It is fundamental to all Christian understanding that God has spoken and that he has spoken in his Son Jesus Christ. One day a student and I were talking about God and his self-revelation, and the student said, "Yes, but when I talk to you, you answer me!" Each of us understands this response, but the fact is that God has indeed answered us, both in words we can read and the Word we can see and know. And this is where we stand or fall as Christians. All our eggs are in this basket.

What if God had not revealed himself and we were alone in our silence and our darkness? That is precisely the working assumption of our secular culture. The only direction in which it can look for self-understanding is backward and inward. Without God there is no place to look but back down the ladder of "evolutionary development" to the primal slime of our beginnings. Apart from him there can only be descriptions of what is observed and projections from what is examined. There is no hope beyond what the human species can make of itself, no resources beyond the human mind and spirit, no recourse in the face of overwhelming odds, but to the weapons, the tools, the abilities, and the dreams of its own devising.

It is small wonder that enormous sums and vast technology are engaged in the almost desperate search for some voice, some intelligence, some word from someone in the universe other than ourselves. Without God we cannot answer our deepest questions and we cannot bear to be alone.

But God is and God speaks. We are not alone, and Someone is in charge here. Moreover, he speaks in the lived-out life of Jesus, revealing his character and purposes. I am sure that for the Hebrews, and for us, the prime concern was not with the existence of God, but with his nature and character. The Word of God has been spoken in a Son, whose life among us meets that concern with the clear revelation that God is like Jesus. Because he has spoken his word, we know who he is. He is the Christlike God.

## • We Know What God Is Like Through the Son

I wonder if any issue is more significant for us than the reality of the Christlike God. I believe that many of our doubts and insecurities, angers and fears have their roots in the unresolved contradictions within our perceptions of the character of God. Our own pictures and images of God are in conflict. We vacillate between the God of justice and the God of love. We waver between the God of law and the God of grace. We know he is like Jesus, but we live under the judgments of a god of our own devising—the composite of the Bible, our parents, our bad experiences, and our good luck. The Hebrews would understand us very well. They, too, were ambivalent—believing in Jesus, yet not quite ready to fully trust that the partial and varied revelations they had experienced through their history were finally and supremely expressed in him.

That is why the letter to the Hebrews is direct and explicit: God has spoken in Jesus Christ his Son, who "reflects the glory of God and bears the very stamp of his nature" (1:3). The point is not that because the Son bears the stamp of the Father, we know what the *Son* is like. It is rather that since the Son bears the stamp of the Father, we know what the *Father* is like. The Father does not reveal the Son; the Son reveals the Father.

The exhortations and warnings of Hebrews are urgent because our understanding of God must come from God's self-revelation. God has spoken and revealed himself. If we begin with God and then say that Jesus is like him, we interpret Jesus in terms of whatever our ideas of God happen to be. The writer of the Hebrews would have us turn things around and look to Jesus to answer our questions of God. We must not turn away from him who speaks "from heaven" (12:25) and create our own false god in our own false image.

This opening word from the Hebrew writer is actually the best and most liberating word we could ever hear. We can know that God is God and that he is not closed off from us. He does not wait for us to seek him, groping in our silent darkness; he takes the initiative to speak to us, to call us to dialogue. He has come to us where we are to reveal himself among us in the person of Jesus Christ. We may respond, we may obey, and we may praise because we know and trust the character of our creator-redeemer God who is like Jesus.

## • We Know the World Through the Son

If we know the character of God through his Son, we also know the character of the world that he has created through his Son. Read the following Scriptures and see how the world comes into being through the Son. He is "the heir of all things, through whom also he created the world, . . . upholding the universe by his word of power" (1:2–3). The same understanding is expressed in the fourth Gospel:

In the beginning was the Word, and the Word was with God, and the Word was God. He was in the beginning with God; all things were made through him, and without him was not anything made that was made (John 1:1-3).

In Colossians, Paul speaks of the "beloved Son" who is

the image of the invisible God, the first-born of all creation; for in him all things were created, in heaven and on earth, visible and invisible, whether thrones or dominions or principalities or authorities—all things were created through him and for him (1:15-16).

These are profound and radical words! They put the activity of the incarnate Word at the center of the creative work of God. I believe the point of each of these Scriptures is the same: the universe is not "spiritual," that is, it is not a mysterious thing governed by strange spiritual forces or angelic beings or heavenly powers, either benign or demonic. It is the direct creation of God through his eternal Son; it is a good creation and Jesus is lord of it.

This was a significant truth for the Hebrews. Like the Colossians (some scholars see important parallels between Hebrews and Colossians), they assumed the existence of angelic beings or forces between the world and God, beings who were to be placated or appeased or manipulated by various practices such as fasting or abstaining from certain foods and observing special days and rituals. Hebrews (and Colossians) cuts straight through such beliefs and declares that the God we know in Jesus Christ his Son is the creator of the worlds. He is lord of the universe. There is no enchanted forest, there is no magic. There are no strange forces or weird beings in the heavens who can exercise influence or control over God's created and redeemed people. At the heart of the universe is not a force, but the Father.

We need this truth as desperately as the Hebrews ever could need it. The first-century world thought in terms of angels and demons and aeons. Our world thinks in terms of scientific laws and forces and structures and technologies; it thinks in terms of economic and sociological principles and historical determinism.

The secular world worships these forces and is surrendered to them. Religious language is not used, but it is idolatry nonetheless.

Furthermore, our industrialized world with its scientific base and its technological application to human life has made persons and personal values less and less significant. We are reduced more and more to units of productivity, which, like machines, are used until worn out, then put aside and replaced. Impersonal law has become all important, and the personal creative activity of God has become totally insignificant. Persons feel more under the control of forces than under the control of the Father and are therefore uncertain and fearful, alienated from the universe and alienated from God.

In such a cultural climate there is increased hunger for some sort of spiritual or transcendent reality, some source of meaning for life. We are seeing an obvious increase in such beliefs as reincarnation, Satan worship, magic, astrology, witchcraft, and mystical religions. Another expression of this "spiritual" hunger is the escapism of drugs, alcohol, extreme rock music, and video fantasies. Yet another is the frenzied quest for money, power, and pleasure. Behind them all, I believe, is the feeling that the world is out of control and there is little to be done to change the self-destructive course of events. We need to know that Jesus is lord of the universe. We are at home in his world, and our end is not the abyss of a black hole. Jesus is Lord.

The Son who is Lord upholds "the universe by his word of power" (1:3). "He is before all things, and in him all things hold together" (Col. 1:17). The "word of power" is not another way of describing the laws of the universe as we understand them. The vision of Christ shared by New Testament Christians did not give them scientific information, but it did give them profound understanding of the nature of the universe. They knew that underneath, sustaining and upholding this universe, is the eternal God, whose likeness and glory are revealed in Jesus Christ our Lord.

This is the "high Christology" of Hebrews, and it speaks directly to our own time. Beneath our skeptical exterior we still wonder, do the stars control us? Are there really spiritual forces in the universe of which we are ignorant, yet which influence our lives? What if we do find life somewhere out there? Are the science fiction writers on to something? Do weird creatures inhabit the marshes of unknown planets? What will happen to us?

It is tremendously important that we know our true source and our true home. There are a million things we do not know, but what we do know outweighs them all. The universe is the creation of God, whose power is not confined to its origins—it is continuously sustained by the word of his power and it will finally be brought to its rightful end. We know this because the God who is creator is also redeemer, ultimately triumphant in his Son over all opposing forces.

Jesus Christ the Son of God is active in creation, lord of creation, and heir of all things. That puts him at the center of reality. In Christ we find meaning for life and fulfillment of life. In him things cohere, hold together, make sense. He is the heir. All things, then—the wealth, the learning, the wisdom, the achievements—all belong to him in the sense that they are the expressions of the divine image in struggling mankind, whose art and vision, whose aspirations and accomplishments reflect, however dully or distortedly, the presence of the Spirit of the Christlike God.

## • We Know Our Sinfulness Through the Son

The supreme revelation of God in Christ also tells us something about our sins. The opening statement of Hebrews is magnificent in its depth and grandeur. No more profound and exalted description of Christ is found in the entire New Testament. The eternal Son is the final revelation of the Father, the heir of all things, agent in creation, reflecting the very nature and glory of God. Then abruptly, before we even get to verse 4, we are confronted with the reality of our sins.

We have a Father's revelation in a magnificent creation, but what does it matter if we cannot be at home in his presence or know any kinship with his holiness? The creation reflects the glory of the Christlike God, but what about our wayward, restless wills without a true home or master? It will matter little to us that the universe is held together by the word of his power if our inner lives are fragmented by guilt and anxiety. "The heavens declare the glory of God," the psalmist says, but what is our glory if our freedom is bound by habits of failure and our hearts stained by the uncleanness of our iniquity?

The good news of the gospel of Hebrews is that our creator is also our redeemer, our Lord is also our high priest, who has made purification for our sins. The Son of God who is heir to the glory of the created worlds is also heir to the shame and defeat, the pain and bitterness, the cruelty and degradation of fallen mankind. It is the awesome reality of the gospel that the one who is reigning Lord is also the one who was "wounded for our transgressions" and "bruised for our iniquities" (Isa. 53:5).

Much more is said about this in the book of Hebrews, but here, at its very beginning, we are told that our sovereign Lord can do what no angels could do, what no prophets nor laws nor priests nor sacrifices could do. We are told what God himself can do; rather, what he has done. Our creator-redeemer has made purification for our sins and has been exalted at the right hand of the majesty on high.

This imagery means that what he has done to redeem us on earth is certified in heaven. The one who is our offering for sin is enthroned with authority in glory. The point is that he has power to forgive and power to cleanse. Words like forgiveness and cleansing are not just nice religious terms; they are realities we may experience. We may be truly forgiven, truly cleansed. In A. M. Hunter's words, God can "cleanse the conscience that has been defiled" and can break "the octopus grip that sin has upon the soul."

The God who in "many and various ways spoke of old to our fathers by the prophets" has "spoken to us by a Son" . . . "in these last days" (1:1–2). "In these last days" is an important phrase. What God has done in Jesus is not something out of the blue. It is the climax of his agelong saving purposes. We have said that there is no enchanted forest, there is no magic, not even for God. He works out his will in his willing creation with his unwilling children through the course of our human history. With infinite love and infinite patience, in judgment and deliverance, by law and ritual, priest and prophet, he has continued his saving work. Then, "when the time had fully come, God sent forth his Son" (Gal. 4:4). He spoke through his Son "in these last days."

These are last days in the sense that the Christ-event is the last in a series of partial and incomplete progressive revelations—the supreme and ultimate revelation of the Father. These days are also last in the sense that the entrance of the incarnate Christ into our world to redeem us inaugurates the last dispensation. Whether we are at the end of the end times or somewhere in the middle of the end times, we are in the last days. The kingdom has been inaugurated, the Messiah has come. The last days are here, and the next great event is the climax, the Second Coming, the consummation. That is the goal toward which we journey as pilgrim people of God.

## ● Conclusion

In Hebrews we learn that our captain is the sovereign Son of God who reflects the Father's nature, mediates the Father's creation, and accomplishes the Father's redemption. He is our prophet who speaks the word of God, he is our priest who makes purification for sins, and he is our king who is exalted at the right hand of the majesty on high.

Above the clamor of the pressing claims of the little gods and the half gods and the no gods, God has spoken. Are we listening?

## ● Discussion Questions

1. Discuss this idea: We don't understand the Son because we understand the Father; rather, we understand the Father precisely

because he has revealed himself in the Son. Do you usually think first of God and then think of Jesus as the Son of God, or do you usually think first of Jesus and then think of God as the Father, his Father?

2. Discuss the idea that Jesus is the "word made flesh," that God "has spoken" in Jesus. Why is God's word so important? This would be a good occasion to look in a concordance for the uses of the phrase "the word of the Lord."

3. Is it enough to say that God is like Jesus? If more is to be said, what is it? How would your ideas of God change if your only way of knowing what he is like came from your understanding of Jesus?

4. Why do you think so many people believe in astrology or the idea that there are powers and forces in the universe that really control our destinies? What are Christians to think about such things? Does the teaching that the Father created the worlds through the Son eliminate belief in such things?

5. Discuss my suggestion that the influence of science and technology has eroded our sense of personal worth and the sense of purpose and meaning in the universe. What do you think about this?

6. Why does the writer speak so early in his "exhortation" (13:22) about the purification for sins (1:3)? What does sin have to do with the fact that the Father created all things?

7. Do the young people you know have a sense of hope for the future, or do the threat of nuclear war and the immense problems of our society lead them to think there really is no future for our world? What are some ways that the idea of Christ as the "heir of all things" relates to this problem?

# C H A P T E R · 3

# Jesus
# Our Brother Now

Therefore we must pay the closer attention to what we have heard, lest we drift away from it. For if the message spoken by angels was valid and every transgression or disobedience received a just retribution, how shall we escape if we neglect such a great salvation? It was declared at first by the Lord, and it was attested to us by those who heard him, while God also bore witness by signs and wonders and various miracles and by gifts of the Holy Spirit distributed according to his own will. . . .

For it was fitting that he, for whom and by whom all things exist, in bringing many sons to glory, should make the pioneer of their salvation perfect through suffering. For he who sanctifies and those who are sanctified have all one origin. That is why he is not ashamed to call them brethren. . . .

Since therefore the children share in flesh and blood, he himself likewise partook of the same nature, that through death he might destroy him who has the power of death, that is, the devil, and deliver all those who through fear of death were subject to lifelong bondage. For surely it is not with angels that he is concerned but with the descendants of Abraham.

Therefore he had to be made like his brethren in every respect, so that he might become a merciful and faithful high priest in the service of God, to make expiation for the sins of the people. For because he himself has suffered and been tempted, he is able to help those who are tempted (Heb. 2:1–4, 10–11, 14–18).

• Hebrews is a book of great theology, strong exhortation, and serious warning. In this passage we hear the first words of exhortation and warning based on the theology of 1:1–4. It is clear that the writer's first concern is not theology for the sake of theology; it is theology for the sake of life. Specifically, he is concerned that his readers find and keep a right view of Christ and the salvation he provides and not let time or trouble or the appeal of other loyalties steal their joy or erode their faithfulness.

## ● The Problem of Drift

This threat to faithfulness was precisely what these Christians had to fear. They had made a radical break with their past. Fresh beginnings were accompanied by joyous emotion and promise. Perhaps there had been a transformation in lifestyle and a great renewal. But years had gone by, and in the way that new love sometimes changes to old marriage, they were cooling off. They were tired of facing the stress of their new commitment in conflict with their old heritage. They began to remember what they had given up and were tempted to reach back into their past and pull into their Christian beliefs elements of their old practices and lifestyles. They were becoming careless and indifferent. Perhaps they had experienced disappointment or hurt and were becoming weary in well-doing. They had failed to grow through the discipline of ordinary Christian life and so had begun the process of degeneration.

The word for it is "drift." It wasn't that they would cease being religious; on the contrary, that is precisely what they would be—religious. They had turned away from the vitality of dynamic personal relationship and were drifting into complacent patterns of self-centered religious behavior.

The warning of Hebrews is strong and clear: Neglect of the great salvation leaves no escape. The exhortation calls us to give closer attention to what we have heard, to listen carefully to the word. It was spoken by the Lord, attested by those who heard, and confirmed by God through miraculous works of the Holy Spirit. The word that has been heard is the word of the God who spoke through his Son in creation, who in many and various ways has revealed himself through his servants and has finally manifested himself in Jesus Christ. That was the saving word, the liberating word, the hopeful word. The matter of hearing the word is crucial because the word spoken is the final word.

We can almost feel the sadness and the urgency of the writer. His readers *must* become attentive and alive again to the reality of the gospel. They *must* see again the glory and the grandeur of Christ, the redeeming Son of God. They *must* become attentive again to the saving word and know that the issues are ultimate and their decisions have eternal consequences. They *must* not drift away and lose it all by default.

What shall we say about ourselves? There is little to be gained by the dreary rehearsal of the processes of our own drift. How many of us in the first days of faith in Christ experienced the joy and liberty and vitality of new relationship, but have experienced the erosion of time and the dulling effect of trouble and disappointment? Other interests and concerns have filled our time and consumed our energies and have sapped the vitality of our faith. Too many of us are drifting away from discipline and loyalty. The routine continues, but hope is gone.

We have all witnessed that pattern. I have talked with students—particularly those who have had radical, emotional conversion or "born-again" experiences—who have said, after a term or two, "Why don't I feel the way I felt when I first came here? Maybe there is nothing to the Christian life after all." The Christian life was so identified with feeling that when emotions subsided, the life itself was threatened.

When Bob came to college, full of joy and enthusiasm for Christ, his mind began to grow and expand. Unfortunately, so did his intellectual pride. Before long he disdained his simple heritage of faith, let go his spiritual disciplines, and found himself adrift, rejecting the very sources of both his spiritual and intellectual life. His lack of discipline took its toll on his whole life. He is going nowhere, doing nothing. How sad this drift!

## ● The Need for Obedience

The real question is, how do we stop the drift? For the Hebrews and for us, the answer is the same. It is the old anticlimactic exhortation: Turn and listen; pay attention to the word you have heard. The problem is that the great word can be heard by our dull and listless ears as the same old familiar word we think we already know.

What we think we want is some new experience, some new gift, some new miracle. What is called for is a radical shift of attention—an energetic and resolute turning away from passive drifting to active response to the relationship into which the living word calls us. It would seem that the grandeur and magnitude of the creative and redeeming word spoken by God in his Son is to be matched by the purposeful and obedient listening of his redeemed people. The word and the response are of equal significance. The word is the saving word; how shall we escape if we neglect it?

Obedience to the word is all the more important because it was spoken by the Son and not by the angels. In Judaism, angels were significant because they were believed to have been the ones through whom the law was given—the law that demanded full obedience. Angels were also thought to have some control over the nations. But "it was not to angels that God subjected the world to come" (2:5).

The comparison of the Son and the angels turns the author's mind to Psalm 8. As you read it, note that this comparison at first appears to be an intrusion into the flow of thought. This is a psalm that celebrates the dignity of man as the creation of God, made a little lower than the angels, fulfilling God's original intention, exercising dominion over the world even as Adam had dominion over the Garden of Eden.

The psalmist shows that in actual fact, in spite of his exalted position, man is never capable of exercising the responsible stewardship of dominion as God intended. Humankind was given both authority and responsibility to have dominion over the created order. That dominion was to be exercised in stewardship, in accountability to God. The misuse of authority and the evasion of responsibility have led to the obvious result: We do not see all things under him. The plain truth is that man is supposed to take care of the world, and he hasn't. Uncontrolled results of his misuse and abuse keep emerging—such things as erosion, land stripping and flooding, contamination seepage and pollution. Our efforts to control our environment by means of our vast technology seem to produce two negative side results for every one positive advancement.

In the meantime, we are witnessing the use of false spiritual powers as a means of controlling and manipulating the world we were charged by God to care for ourselves! For all our human capability, we certainly do not see all things put under our dominion.

But we see another man "who was made a little lower than the angels;" it is Jesus! The writer to the Hebrews sees Jesus as the one, the only one, who actually reflects the created grandeur that man was intended to have and that angels could never have. He is the embodiment of humanity as it ought to be. He is the "last Adam," who expresses the dignity and the dominion that the first Adam was supposed to have but lost because of sin. Through his death Jesus makes possible the recovery of fallen man's lost glory. He who was higher than the angels became lower than the angels to bring men to the fulfillment of their otherwise lost destiny. His humiliation and his suffering are his glory and our salvation.

Look at Psalm 8: It expresses the grandeur of man.

Look at Hebrews: It expresses the misery of man. "We do not yet see everything in subjection to him" (2:8).

Then look at Jesus: He endures the misery to bring man back to his grandeur!

Chapter 2 begins with a solemn exhortation and warning based on the word of God spoken through his sovereign Son. This Son is the heir of all things, the agent of creation, and the upholder of the universe. Having made purification for our sins, he is seated at the right hand of the majesty on high.

The dominant theme is divine sovereignty, but the chapter closes on the theme of divine humiliation. The divine Son through whom we are created is the one through whom we are redeemed. God in Jesus has undertaken the task of redeeming mankind, and in the process Jesus is revealed as the brother of us all. He has entered utterly into our human situation and endured the misery to bring us back to God. He is our savior, who in his suffering is involved with us as our pioneer and trailblazer. He has submitted to all the conditions under which his brothers and sisters live.

## • Jesus Is Our Brother in Suffering

Jesus indeed knows about suffering, "for it was fitting that he, for whom and by whom all things exist, in bringing many sons to glory, should make the pioneer of their salvation perfect through suffering" (2:10). There is in this verse a contradictory combination of terms. The one who is the creator and sustainer of the universe accomplishes salvation by means of suffering. This is the major offense of the Christian gospel. It was then and it is now.

The hard thing for the Hebrews to accept was that Christ was higher than the angels, yet he was made lower than the angels, entered fully into the human situation, into the "arena of anguish," and suffered. Far from explaining or excusing, the writer declares that sharing the suffering of humanity is the very means by which the sovereign Son of God saves us.

In Hebrews 2:9, Christ suffers death, tasting it for everyone. In 2:18, he suffers temptation. In 5:8, the prayers, tears, and loud cries of the Son of God reveal the depth of the suffering through which he learned obedience. In 13:12, Jesus suffers outside the gate to sanctify us.

The writer is also keenly aware of the suffering endured by the Hebrews. They had been publicly exposed to abuse and afflictions because of their faith in Christ. In 2:10, the phrase "it was fitting" is used in connection with the creator's work of redemption. The writer saw that it was appropriate that the savior suffer in the process of bringing his followers into the splendor of their salvation.

Two dimensions to Christ's sufferings are implied in Hebrews 2. One is that the people Jesus came to save know the meaning of suffering. Life is difficult and suffering is inevitable. When God spoke to Moses through the burning bush, he said, "I have seen the affliction of my people . . . and have heard their cry. . . . I know their sufferings, and I have come down to deliver them" (Exod. 3:7–8).

The long journey of the people of God is one of hurt and trouble and suffering. For that matter, the long journey of all mankind on this earth has been marked by pain and suffering. We are consumed with the avoidance of it. It would seem to be the main business of modern religion to avoid suffering. Everything we hear through the public media promises us health and happiness, fulfillment of our desires, and deliverance from trouble and sorrow. But all our false declarations are vain. Our deceptive religious formulas are ineffectual. We are creatures who suffer.

There is no explanation of our suffering in Hebrews—nor of Jesus'. It is simply and profoundly affirmed that he is the one who suffers with us. In our suffering we cannot keep from asking why. Nor could Jesus on the cross! His answer was not an explanation, but the assurance of his Father's presence. Hebrews offers no explanation, either, but assures us of the presence of our pioneer and captain who experiences and understands our suffering.

The second dimension of suffering is found in the term variously translated "pioneer," "captain," "author," "princely leader," "ruler," "originator," "founder of their salvation" (2:10). Obviously the original Greek word has many shades of meaning, but as applied to Christ, they all imply that Jesus has come to where we are, has entered fully into our suffering human situation, and leads us on our journey. Angels may observe, but if the Son is to overcome our alienation, he must come and personally participate in the situation of those he reconciles. He is our pilgrim leader, our pioneer who has entered into the reality of our human condition. He did not shrink from the inevitable suffering.

He walked the trail, knows the hurts and the pains of the journey, and with compassion and empathy leads us to final triumph.

Our pioneer is made "perfect" in his suffering. The meaning is not that his moral character needed improvement. This is made clear in 7:26: "It was fitting that we should have such a high priest, holy, blameless, unstained, separated from sinners, exalted above the heavens." His suffering is part of the completion of his saving work; he couldn't be the perfect pioneer, the perfect captain of our salvation, without it. Can we see what this tells us about the way God is present with us in the saving process? Can we know that he enters into our sufferings and knows our weakness and our hurt? Our pioneer is our brother.

## • Jesus Is Our Brother in Temptation

Jesus also knows about temptation. "Therefore he had to be made like his brethren in every respect, so that he might become a merciful and faithful high priest in the service of God, to make expiation for the sins of the people. For because he himself has suffered and been tempted, he is able to help those who are tempted. . . . For we have not a high priest who is unable to sympathize with our weaknesses, but one who in every respect has been tempted as we are, yet without sin" (2:17–18; 4:15).

How is it possible for us to think that Christ was tempted the same way we are? We think of his divinity and his purity in ways that isolate him from the real world where temptation and suffering are actual and urgent. It is hard for us to accept it, but Hebrews makes it clear: He suffered, being tempted in every respect as we are. It cannot mean, of course, that Jesus experienced the same specific temptations we do. He did not know the stress and temptations a woman knows, or the problems and adjustments of marriage and family. He was never elderly, nor did he live in a scientific age. The assurance the Hebrew writer wants to give is that the Christ we have come to trust is like us in every way. He did not face our particular temptations, but he met the full range of temptation.

We wonder how one so sinless as Jesus could understand the meaning of temptation as we, who know so much about sin and failure, experience it. Actually Jesus knows more about temptation than we do. The one who lives in immorality does not know the price of purity. The one who follows the whims and desires of the hour does not understand the price of discipline. In a similar way Christ understands the full force of temptation in ways that we never could. We have yielded before its full force has been exercised. The losing wrestler does not know the full power of his opponent. It is the one who wins who has experienced the total force of his opponent's strength. It is Jesus who really knows the power of Satan. He has felt the full weight of his opposing strength and has triumphed. He knows how powerful temptation can be.

### • Jesus Is Our Brother When We Fail

The point is not to prove that Jesus did not sin in the stress of his testings; rather, it is to reveal the depth of his sympathy with those who struggle with temptation and fall. The warnings at the beginning of chapter 2 called the Hebrews to renewed attentiveness, renewed grip and spirit, new heart and enthusiasm, and recovery of the joy of first love.

Perhaps the writer knew that underneath their drift and loss of nerve were secret hurts and failures, hidden burdens and defeats. Very few believers choose to drift; seldom do Christians plan to be lukewarm. But poor performance undermines confidence and failure causes discouragement. Temptation, even when overcome, leaves us battle-scarred and weary. It is sometimes difficult to tell the difference between victory and defeat because issues are never clear-cut and our successes never total. When one has struggled through the testing time and finally endured, it seldom feels like triumph.

At such times—as the Hebrew writer knew—we desperately

need to know that Jesus is our brother, with us as we struggle on the way, having the compassion that can only come through his shared experience of suffering and temptation. Our approach to the throne of grace (4:16) is not on the basis of our victories. We are not invited because we are worthy. Jesus our brother opens up the way for us to come in our weaknesses, temptations, and failures. He is with us in sympathy and help, not at the end of our struggle, but all the way through.

This is the only way, I believe, that we can maintain vitality and energy and joy in the long haul of the Christian life. Someone has to help us *at the time of our struggle;* we need help *while we are trying;* we need a brother *in the hour of trial,* and especially when we fail. Otherwise we fall into the discouragement of trying harder or of never quite measuring up. The subtle shift from trust in Christ to our own self-efforts robs us of hope and joy. We begin to tally hurts, count disappointments, and weigh sacrifices. And already the drift has set in. We need the warning, but more than that, we need to know that we are known, understood, and loved by someone who has marked out the path, has won the victory, and is with us on the way. That someone is Jesus.

## • Jesus Is Our Brother in the Face of Death

Jesus knows about suffering, he knows about temptation, and he knows about death. "Since therefore the children share in flesh and blood, he himself likewise partook of the same nature, that through death he might destroy him who has the power of death, that is, the devil, and deliver all those who through fear of death were subject to lifelong bondage" (2:14–15). Much is said through the rest of Hebrews about the death of Jesus our high priest. What is said here only reveals the depth of his identification with us in our mortality. Our ultimate suffering, our ultimate test, and our ultimate failure is our experience of death.

What is our source of renewal if death is the end? How can we find again the vitality of first love if the fear of death hangs over us? In experiencing death Christ robbed it of its power to control and stifle us. He is the priest who shares our life and death—and so delivers us from the fear of death. That fear has no magical power. It is nothing we cannot confront with faith and trust because one we know and trust has already gone through it. He gives us courage and help as we walk our own way toward our inevitable end, which, because of him, is no longer a frightening darkness but the doorway to new life in glory. Jesus our brother is with us all the way.

## ● Conclusion

Jesus' humiliation, suffering, and death reveal something significant about the way God acts in him to save us. It is important to know where God is when he saves us. He is not far off, dealing with us by divine powers from some heavenly realm. He has come to where we are in Jesus, has taken up the journey with us, and has saved us from "inside" our humanity and frailty. God has come in Jesus to share with us, experience what we experience, and mark out the way for us.

The writer says it is "fitting" for Jesus, our pioneer and priest, to be human as we are. That is, it is all right for Jesus to be human. That is how he knows us, that is how he is able to be sympathetic with us, that is why he can truly save us from our real selves in our sinful, human condition. If it is all right for Jesus to be human, then it is all right for us to be human, too. We are not saved by becoming divine or being strong or right. We are not called to transcend our humanity to approach God. We are saved by responding in faith to the one who is not ashamed to call us brothers. We are called to walk with the one who walks with us in our humanity to bring us to glory.

## ● Discussion Questions

1. What are some of the changes that go along with the passing of the honeymoon stage of Christian living and experience? What are some differences between a "normal" loss of excitement and the kind of drifting the writer to the Hebrews warns against?
2. Based on your experience, what are some causes of drift?
3. People in Bible times thought in terms of angels and powers controlling the world and controlling themselves. Those terms are still sometimes used, but what other words are used today to describe those powers? What is the appeal of astrology or reincarnation?
4. Could it be that some people's desire for the Second Coming is more a desire for escape from the awful problems we have created for ourselves than a desire for the triumph of the kingdom? What is wrong with the prayer, "O Lord, things are awful, take us home to be with you"?
5. The book of Hebrews shows plainly both Jesus' divinity and his humanity. Which is easier for us to affirm? Why?
6. I believe it is good for us to reflect on the tragic dimension of life and its suffering and pain. Discuss the idea that the public media, both religious and secular, have distorted our perspective and enticed us into a false world of happiness, health, and trouble-free pleasure.
7. How can Jesus be tempted? Can one who never sinned really know more about the power of temptation than we do? Explain.
8. It is all right for Jesus to be human. That means it is all right for us to be human, too. What do you think of the idea that we are not called to deny or transcend our humanity to be saved? Can we affirm our humanity without approving sin?

# CHAPTER · 4

# Consider Jesus

Therefore, Holy brethren, who share in a heavenly call, consider Jesus, the apostle and high priest of our confession. He was faithful to him who appointed him, just as Moses also was faithful in God's house. Yet Jesus has been counted worthy of as much more glory than Moses as the builder of a house has more honor than the house. . . . Now Moses was faithful in all God's house as a servant, to testify to the things that were to be spoken later, but Christ was faithful over God's house as a son. And we are his house if we hold fast our confidence and pride in our hope (Heb. 3:1–3, 5–6).

● The intent of the letter to the Hebrews is the encouraging of discouraged Christians. This goal is achieved by lifting up Jesus— showing how his relationship with God places him in a relationship with humanity far superior to that of any other being or person or power, no matter how exalted or influential. His appeal is both simple and profound: "Consider Jesus!"

At the beginning of the letter, Jesus is seen in relation to the prophets through whom God spoke in times past. He is then compared with angels through whom God gave the revelation and who were thought to have power both with nature and the nations. Now the writer begins to compare Jesus the Son with Moses the servant, the one through whom the law was given to Israel.

## ● Brothers With Christ

The address "Holy brethren" points right to the superiority of the relationship with God that Jesus established for the Hebrews. They are holy brothers, not because they have struggled through the legalistic system and have achieved holiness, but because Christ has entered human life and has overcome mankind's alienation from God. As priest he has brought them to God and they have by faith become part of the community of saints, the called of God who belong to him.

Jesus does what the Mosaic law could never do. For all his faithfulness, Moses was still called a servant. For all their faithlessness, the Hebrews to whom this letter was addressed were still called brethren, because Jesus the Son became their brother. He reconciled them and brought them into the household of God. He has reconciled us and made us brothers as well. We are no more able to achieve our own standing before God than they. We are privileged to belong to the "holy brethren" only because Jesus is our brother and our priest. He has atoned for our sin and brought us into a holy relationship with God.

The Hebrews are brothers who share "a heavenly calling." In 6:4, the writer speaks of the "heavenly gift," which he connects with the Holy Spirit, and in 8:5, of the "heavenly sanctuary," which is compared with the earthly tabernacle. In 9:23, the sacrificial rites are copies of "heavenly things." The faith heroes of chapter 11 "desire a better country, that is, a heavenly one" (v. 16), and those who share the new covenant have come, not to Sinai, but "to Mount Zion and to the city of the living God, the heavenly Jerusalem" (12:23). The word is used in contrast to what is earthly, what is unreal, and what is transient.

The call is from heaven, not from earth, and it calls the Hebrews away from the unreality and transience of this world's life and values. Finally, at the end of the journey, it calls them to heaven. The word also indicates the sovereign authority of Jesus, "the apostle and high priest" through whom the call is given. His "heavenly" place and status give him power over all the forces or beings that would seduce the Hebrews from their loyal participation in the call of God. They have no need to fear or draw back. They share in a call that has its source in God and is given with the power and grace of God.

God's world has confronted our world in the word of Jesus, our apostle. He comes all the way into our alienated and impotent humanity, identifies utterly with us, and calls us into conversation with him. This is an important idea in the book of Hebrews. The letter itself is called a "word of exhortation" (13:22). It begins with reference to the many and various ways God spoke in times past and has now spoken in Jesus his Son (1:1−2). God says things to the angels and to the Son (1:5−14). We are urged to give attention to what we have heard from the Lord (2:1−3). The Holy Spirit speaks (3:7), and we are to exhort one another (3:13). We are to hear the divinely spoken word with the kind of faith that guarantees reception and consequent benefit for our lives (4:2). There is much to be said to us, but we are dull of hearing (5:11).

We must not forget the exhortation that speaks to us as sons, and we must not refuse him who speaks from heaven (12:5, 25). God from heaven comes to earth in his Son and calls us into dialogue. That dialogue is salvation. It is the author's way of expressing a saving relationship with God. God's word confronts us with the call to respond, to listen, to pay attention (which is faith), and so be caught up in the saving dialogue. Attentive response to the divine word brings us into a relationship with God that is far superior to anything the law or the rituals of the old dispensation could possibly provide.

● Conversation With God

In the New Testament there are many different ways of expressing or describing our relationship with God. In the first three Gospels Jesus calls the people to repent and enter the kingdom, that is, come under the kingly rule of God as revealed in Jesus. In the Gospel of John we are told we experience eternal life when we believe in the name of the Son of God. In the Epistles Paul speaks of righteousness or right relationship with God through faith in the reconciling death of Jesus. In Hebrews the relationship is described in terms of dialogue with God through Jesus.

When someone speaks to us and we respond and enter into conversation, a relationship develops. The exchange of words carries an exchange of thoughts and feelings and intentions. We are mutually affected by the dialogue. The insights and experiences of the other person influence how we think and what we do. As the dialogue continues and deepens, so does the relationship. In fact, the relationship that develops can itself be described as "conversational" or "dialogical."

In Hebrews, God takes the initiative and begins the dialogue with mankind, speaking in various ways "to our fathers by the prophets." What actually made Israel unique among the nations was that it was the nation *to* whom God spoke and the nation *through* whom God intended to speak to the rest of the world.

In these last days, God has spoken in his Son. He has begun a personal conversation, calling us to respond and enter into the dialogue. Our entering into the conversation pulls the whole of our lives into relationship with God. We find ourselves involved with him, responding to his will, and participating in his purposes. The relationship is kept energetic and vital as we are attentive and receptive to the movement of the dialogue. When we grow listless and careless and become distracted, we drift, and the relationship cools and is threatened. As we come back to attention and response, entering wholeheartedly into the conversation, motivation is restored and new life is kindled.

Sometimes the conversation exposes our drift and our danger of pulling back. It confronts our disengagement and apathy. At such times we need to look again to Jesus, to consider again the majesty and the glory of his person and become attentive again to his word. We need to pay the more earnest heed to what we have heard, to engage again in the divine dialogue that alone can save us. This is a significant and helpful way of thinking of our relationship with God in Jesus and what it means to live the Christian life.

## ● Dynamic Communion

The exhortations throughout Hebrews to pay attention, to listen, and to give ear to the saving word, all let us know that the relationship to which we are called is not static. We are not placed in a "state" of grace or spirituality in which we may rest secure. We are in dynamic communion, in continuing dialogue with the God who initiates conversation that is continually renewed. If our ears grow dull and we become listless, we fail to be attentive to the spoken word. We then become vulnerable to the influence of other voices and other calls.

The author of Hebrews takes his place in a long line of divinely called spokesmen—a line still lengthening—who exhort the people of God to give heed to the saving word. Israel's basic confession of faith in Deuteronomy 6:4 begins, "Hear, O Israel: The LORD our God is one LORD." "Hear" in this case does not mean something like "behold." It means "listen, pay attention, give heed, respond." The call of the prophets to Israel was, "Hear the word of the LORD" (Isa. 1:10; Jer. 2:4; Amos 3:1). How often Jesus said in his parables, "He who has ears, let him hear" (Matt. 13). Peter began his message on the Day of Pentecost with the familiar formula, "Give ear to my words" (Acts 2:14). In Revelation we are urged to "hear what the Spirit says to the churches" (2:7, 11, 17, 29; 3:6, 13, 22).

In each case what is called for is not passive hearing; it is not agreement or even understanding; it is active and attentive response. It is the kind of listening that includes the mind and heart and will and issues in obedient following. The conversation into which God in Jesus calls us is the "stuff," the content, the heart of our relationship with him. Our Christian lives are characterized by continual, dynamic attentiveness to the voice and the word of God.

When we cease listening to our own wayward hearts and stop paying attention to the voices of the world and respond to the call of God, we are placed in inevitable tension both with ourselves and with our world. The word of God does not call us out of the world into a realm of spiritual existence that transcends the world. Jesus, the spoken Word, has come in real incarnation into our genuine humanity in this secular world and has called us to belong to him.

We are, then, not of the world, but we are in it (John 17:11–16). Like the Hebrews, we are "holy brethren" who are yet in the world, sharing the life and the temptations and the struggles of the world. But there is a call upon us; it is the incessant, loving, whispering, thundering, warning, encouraging, heavenly call of God. It is a call that constrains us to cease our dialogue with the world, disengage the emotional attachments of our worldly conversation, and respond to the divine life-giving word.

## • Pilgrimage With God

As we respond to God's word to us and open ourselves to the conversation he has initiated, we discover it is not an exercise in parlor talk. The dialogue into which we are called leads to pilgrimage. Our participation in conversation with God involves us in a journey with him and with others who like us have responded to his call.

This is another important understanding of the Christian life described in the letter to the Hebrews. The word we hear with our ears and receive in our hearts moves our feet as well. It constrains us to rise and walk with the people of God. Those to whom Hebrews was written had indeed heard the call, had entered the dialogue, and had begun the journey, but they were getting tired and discouraged. They were growing listless and inattentive. Strong words called them back to the vision of Jesus, the center of the dialogue and the journey. "Therefore, Holy brethren, who share in a heavenly call, consider Jesus, the apostle and high priest of our confession" (3:1).

The exhortation is for them—and for us. "In the midst of your journey consider Jesus." To "consider Jesus" means more than just to look at him; it means to look closely, to think about, and to be attentive to him. In the world and not of it, participating in it and yet alien to it, we find our strength and motivation to continue our journey as we consider Jesus, the faithful Son of God.

Jesus' faithfulness is held up before us in 3:1–6, and it is shown in comparison with Moses, the faithful servant. Let's look at Moses. His faithful parents hid him in the reeds at the river's edge and saved him from the Pharaoh's edict of death; his faithful mother taught and shared the ancestral faith with him during his early years in the royal Egyptian court. His own faith was violently affirmed in his encounter with an oppressing Egyptian taskmaster. It matured during the quiet years in Midian and expressed itself in his obedience to the call of God at Mount Horeb.

In faithful obedience Moses faced the mighty Pharaoh in Egypt. By faith he led his people through their first Passover and across the sea to freedom. For all his humanness, what a faithful and loyal person he was! When his people fell into idolatry and apostasy at the foot of Sinai, Moses responded to God's threat of their destruction with the words, "O Lord GOD, destroy not thy people and thy heritage, whom thou hast redeemed through thy greatness, whom thou hast brought out of Egypt with a mighty hand. Remember thy servants, Abraham, Isaac and Jacob; do not regard the stubbornness of this people, or their wickedness, or their sin" (Deut. 9:26–27). In the face of the great sin of the people, Moses prayed, "But now, if thou wilt forgive their sin— and if not, blot me, I pray thee, out of thy book which thou hast written" (Exod. 32:32).

## ● Greater Than Moses

What a very special sort of person! He was called to bring a nation into existence, but he wasn't the center of that nation. He was called to establish a new religion, but unlike any other great religion, it was not called after his name. He gave laws and spoke immortal words, but they were not his laws or his words; they were the laws and the words of the Lord. What a faithful servant!

Look at Moses with the people of God. They were a people whose very existence and divine destiny depended on his faithful obedience to God and his faithful care for them. He was, indeed, "faithful in all God's house as a servant" (3:5).

Now look at Jesus the faithful Son. He is not compared with the weakness and disloyalty of Moses, but is shown to be superior to the one who was the supreme example of loyalty and faithfulness in the Old Testament. In many ways the Gospels present Jesus as the new and greater Moses who brings about an Exodus for his people far more real and abiding than the passing from Egypt. Jesus was, like Moses, born under an edict of death and delivered by the faithfulness of his parents. He, too, spent time in the land of Egypt. He, too, heard the call of God and was tested in the wilderness. He, too, went in obedience to encounter the might of the prevailing empire with the power of the word of the Lord. He, too, brings together a people of God, the new Israel of faith.

Look at him, and consider him. In faithfulness he speaks the words of his Father: "I have not spoken on my own authority; the Father who sent me has himself given me commandment what to say and what to speak" (John 12:49). In total dependency he does the works of his Father: "The Son can do nothing of his own accord but only what he sees the Father doing" (John 5:19). The faithful Son does nothing on his own authority: "I seek not my own will but the will of him who sent me. . . . I have come down from heaven, not to do my own will, but the will of him who sent me" (John 5:30; 6:38).

One with the Father, the Son goes about doing good, teaching, preaching, and healing. He is faithful through rising opposition and increasing rejection. Alone in Gethsemane he is faithful. At his trial he bears "witness to the truth" (John 18:37). Finally, on the cross, God-abandoned and derelict, the faithful Son prays, "Father, into thy hands I commit my spirit!" (Luke 23:46).

"Consider Jesus! Look at him, pay attention to him!" See that mighty exodus which he accomplishes on the cross by which the new people of God are gathered. Consider him risen from the dead, exalted in power and glory at the right hand of God the Father. Look at the outpouring of the Holy Spirit at Pentecost, certifying the lordship of Jesus.

Can we see Jesus in the midst of the congregation of the people of God? Can we see him as our pioneer and captain, leading the pilgrim people of God on their journey of faith? He is the faithful Son who is head of the gathered body, the "holy brethren" from every tribe and nation and tongue; all peoples from all centuries from all places on our globe. Jesus is with his people. Their very existence as a people and their destiny are totally dependent on his faithfulness to his Father and to them. He is the faithful Son. He will not forsake his gathered people; he will not forget or give up. He is obedient. He is faithful to his Father, he is faithful to his task, and he is faithful to us. The exhortation is strong and clear: "Think about that! Set your mind on that! Consider Jesus!"

## ● The Promised Messiah

Moses was faithful in God's house as a servant, "but Christ was faithful over God's house as a son. And we are his house if we hold fast our confidence and pride in our hope" (3:6). This is the first time the term "Christ" ("Messiah") is used in Hebrews. As Messiah, Jesus fulfills the promise implicit in the role of Moses. He accomplished the saving purposes of God and gathered the new community of faith.

An astounding declaration is made in connection with the work of Christ as faithful over God's house: "We are his house." The plain truth is declared that the church replaces Israel. Israel as such no longer belongs to the household of God. The Messiah has come and has fulfilled the agelong saving purposes of God. He was rejected by Israel as a nation, but the promises made "to our fathers through the prophets" are not lost. They are, in fact, open to the whole world, to all who respond to the call of God who has spoken "in these last days" by his Son, Jesus, the Messiah.

The household of God is not constituted of any special nation or group. It is made up of the children of God by faith, "who were born, not of blood nor of the will of the flesh nor of the will of man, but of God" (John 1:13). The task of Moses the servant was preparatory and promissory. All the long history of salvation recorded in the Old Testament—so familiar to the Hebrews—came to fulfillment and completion in the life, ministry, death, resurrection, and exaltation of Jesus Christ the Son. The people of God, the household of God, are those who hear the word spoken in the Son and respond in attentive listening, who in obedience rise to join the pilgrimage of faith.

"And we are his house if we hold fast our confidence and pride in our hope" (3:6). If the Jews as such do not belong to the household of God, neither are we guaranteed permanent belonging if we do not hold fast our confidence and our hope. In the Son we have free and confident access to God and joyful fellowship with him. We enjoy the openness and freedom of a relationship as brothers and sisters of the Son. But being in God's household means participating in a dialogue that is continually renewed. It means taking part in a conversation that will continue into tomorrow and tomorrow, until the journey's end in final victory.

## • Conclusion

The word to the Hebrews is the exhortation all of us in the household of God need to hear: "Consider Jesus the faithful Son, and hang on to the relationship with God we have in him."

## • Discussion Questions

1. The ones to whom Hebrews was written were not perfect in either character or maturity. What, then, is meant by the address "holy brethren"? In what sense is the church "holy"?

2. Discuss the idea that the writer to the Hebrews pictures the Christian life as a conversation or dialogue. In what ways is it helpful? not helpful?

3. In Hebrews 3 we are called to consider Jesus. From your perspective, what does this mean? Check other translations of 3:1. How are we to respond to this exhortation?

4. What is gained by comparing Jesus with Moses? What do you think is the writer's purpose in making the comparison?

5. As you think about Jesus, what about him is most helpful for you in your Christian life?

6. I have suggested that we need to put more emphasis on the faithfulness of Jesus as our leader and pioneer. Discuss this idea. Do we emphasize too much our need to try to be faithful? Does Hebrews emphasize one more than the other? If so, which?

7. Look up Hebrews 3:6 in other translations and put the verse into your own words.

# CHAPTER · 5

# Rest That Remains

Therefore, as the Holy Spirit says,
"Today, when you hear his voice,
do not harden your hearts as in the rebellion,
on the day of testing in the wilderness,
where your fathers put me to the test
and saw my works for forty years.
Therefore I was provoked with that generation,
and said, 'They always go astray in their hearts;
they have not known my ways.'
As I swore in my wrath,
'They shall never enter my rest.'"

Take care, brethren, lest there be in any of you an evil, unbelieving heart, leading you to fall away from the living God. But exhort one another every day, as long as it is called "today," that none of you may be hardened by the deceitfulness of sin. For we share in Christ if only we hold our first confidence firm to the end. . . .

Since therefore it remains for some to enter it, and those who formerly received the good news failed to enter because of disobedience, again he sets a certain day, "Today," saying through David so long afterward, . . .

"Today, when you hear his voice,
do not harden your hearts."

For if Joshua had given them rest, God would not speak later of another day. So then, there remains a sabbath rest for the people of God; for whoever enters God's rest also ceases from his labors as God did from his.

Let us therefore strive to enter that rest, that no one fall by the same sort of disobedience. For the word of God is living and active, sharper than any two-edged sword, piercing to the division of soul and spirit, of joints and marrow, and discerning the thoughts and intentions of the heart (Heb. 3:7–15; 4:6–12).

● The book of Hebrews describes the people of God as a pilgrim people on a journey to their promised inheritance. The great model of the pilgrim journey is Israel's experience of deliverance from Egypt and their exodus under Moses into the promised land of Canaan. Canaan was the land of their inheritance; it was the land of rest. God said to Moses, "My presence will go with you, and I will give you rest" (Exod. 33:14).

The promise of the Exodus was rest in the land of Canaan under the rule of God. That meant life in freedom, security from enemies, and enjoyment of the bounties of God's gifts in peace. It also meant life expressed in worship and praise to God. It was for the purpose of worship that they departed from Egypt in the first place (Exod. 5:1).

The gift of the land was intended to be experienced as rest and expressed in worship. "But when you go over the Jordan, and live in the land which the LORD your God gives you to inherit, and when he gives you rest from all your enemies round about, so that you live in safety, then to the place which the LORD your God will choose, to make his name dwell there, thither you shall bring all that I command you: your burnt offerings and your sacrifices, your tithes and the offerings that you present . . . And you shall rejoice before the LORD your God" (Deut. 12:10–12).

But those Israelites never did truly enter into the rest provided for them. Before they ever got to the Promised Land, while still in the wilderness, they doubted the presence of God and rebelled against the providence of God. They fell into unbelief and disobedience, and their hearts were hardened. Their vision became so blurred and dimmed they could wish for the old life in Egypt again. Because they drew back from the journey, their whole generation perished.

The next generation did little better. They finally possessed the land, but never did experience in any permanent way the peace, the security, and the relationship that was to be theirs as God's people. The promise of rest was given, but it was not experienced.

In a later century, during the time of the monarchy, the psalmist saw an attitude among his own people that reminded him of his ancestors in the wilderness who missed the rest because of their hardness of heart. He also heard the voice of the Holy Spirit and understood that the ancient promise of rest, though unfulfilled, was God-given and still alive in his own day for his own people. His cry to them was, "O that today you would hearken to his voice! Harden not your hearts, as at Meribah, as on the day at Massah in the wilderness" (Ps. 95:7–8; see Exod. 17:1–7).

But the psalmist's generation followed the example of their forefathers and no more experienced the promised rest than they—and for the same reasons. The saving word was spoken and they had heard it, but what they heard was not mixed with faith on their part. The word and their faith were not stirred together enough to change the quality or the color of their lives. They hardened their hearts, doubted the presence of God, and had no regard for his ways (Ps. 95:8–11). The promise of rest was given again, but it was not experienced.

Still later, the author of Hebrews, now in the day of grace ushered in by the coming of Christ, perceived among his Christian brothers and sisters the same old destructive attitudes and behaviors that had characterized the Israelites in the wilderness and Canaan. Like their forefathers, the Hebrews had heard the word spoken to them, had responded in faith, had entered into dialogue with the gospel, and had begun the pilgrim journey. But the discouragement and drag of the march were getting to them. They were losing heart and losing faith. In spite of all the saving benefits of God's final revelation in Christ, they were yielding to the spirit of rebellion.

## ● The Day of Grace

One can feel the intensity of concern the writer has for his readers. They are precious to him, and he cannot bear for them to fall back, miss the way, and fail to enter into God's promised rest.

In the "today" of the wilderness period the Spirit summoned Israel, in spite of disobedience and rebellion, to trustful rest in the land of God's provision and protection. In the "today" of the monarchy period the Spirit was still faithful, calling the nation to respond in loyalty to the promise of security and peaceful rest.

Though Israel did not hear the word in faith and so did not, in fact, receive the promise, God appointed another day. It is the great "today" of grace, the "today" of the gospel, inaugurated by the word of God spoken through his Son. The Holy Spirit is still saying, "Today, when you hear his voice, do not harden your hearts" (3:7). The promise endures, the one who promises is faithful, and the rest remains—and so does the warning. The readers of Hebrews were living in the day of salvation, the great "today" of grace. They were in danger of doing just as their ancestors had done. They were pulling back from dialogue with God and risked losing the promised sabbath rest.

Our day is a different one from the day of those first-century Christians who first read the book of Hebrews. And yet it is not. The God who spoke to the fathers by the prophets in the yesterdays of history, has spoken to us through his Son, inaugurating the great "today" of grace. It is the "today" of the gospel era, the final "day" of salvation history. It is the day that began with the supreme revelation of God in Jesus and will close with the consummation of the kingdom at the end of the age when he comes again.

This is the day of our journey, and in the course of it we are as vulnerable to drifting back and pulling back as the Hebrews ever were. Our tendency is to imitate our ancestors just as they did. So the message of Hebrews comes to us with warning and encouragement. There is a sabbath rest that remains for us—let us strive to enter it!

## ● The Sabbath Rest

A look at some words and phrases used in chapters 3 and 4 will help to define the rest that remains for the people of God. "Rest" (3:11) is described in 3:14 as participating or sharing in Christ. In 4:1–2, the promise of entering into rest is dependent on believing the "good news." The "rest" of previous generations was an anticipation of the rest made possible by God's spoken word through Christ and the gospel. "Gospel rest" is the experience of a dynamic faith relationship with him. "So we see that they were unable to enter because of unbelief" (3:19), but "we who have believed enter that rest" (4:3). It is a partnership that continues as we "hold our first confidence firm to the end" (3:14).

In 4:9, the words "sabbath rest" occur. They mark an important transition in the development of the author's thought. He speaks of the rest promised to the Israelites in the wilderness and the rest promised to the nation in David's time. But when he speaks of the promise still available to believers in the gospel era, the term is not "rest," but "sabbath rest." His vision reaches back beyond the rest of Canaan to the very Sabbath of God, who rested after the work of creation was complete. "So God blessed the seventh day and hallowed it, because on it God rested from all his work which he had done in creation" (Gen. 2:3).

Sabbath rest relates to the rest of God himself. This was the real rest that Israel missed through their disobedience in the old days, and that the readers of Hebrews were in danger of missing (4:3). "So then, there remains a sabbath rest for the people of God" (4:9). Rest, as sharing in God's own rest, is not something of our making or achieving. We do not enter it by disciplining our time or by exercises of relaxation or meditation, however beneficial these may be.

Creation rest is God given and God centered. It is God's rest into which we enter. It is not that as he comes to help us be more tranquil; we participate in his rest. He rested at the completion of creation, not because he was exhausted after a hard week's work, but because the work was completed. God's rest, however, does not mean the end of activity. Jesus said, "My father is working still, and I am working" (John 5:17). God continues his work of upholding and redeeming the universe he has created.

For the Israelites in Canaan, the weekly round of Sabbaths reflected the rest of God and celebrated the completion of his creative work. Sabbath also celebrated their entrance into the land that had been promised as their inheritance. Their very presence in the land and enjoyment of its bounty testified to the grace of God in their behalf. Dwelling in Canaan was itself a sabbath experience of rest.

## ● Security in Relationship

In the new age of the gospel, rest does not mean security in God's land as much as it means security in a relationship with God. The significance of land, however, is not lost, even though it does not refer specifically to geography. For the Israelites, the possession of the land was directly related to their heart relationship with God. The issues were not social or political or military; they were religious, through and through. Whether or not they possessed the land depended totally on the quality of their obedience to God, their heart loyalty to him, and their trust. Their arms and strategy are not mentioned. They did not fail to enter rest because they were poor or ill-equipped fighters, but rather they hardened their hearts and rebelled and became disobedient.

We can see why the author of Hebrews found in the term "sabbath rest" a rich resource for the message of encouragement and warning he had for his readers. "Sabbath rest" was a good term to express the kind of rest they were to have in their relationship with God. It was a rest illustrated by the old custom of Sabbath in the Promised Land. Sabbath rest, then, means being secure and at peace in the place of God's provision, living under his protection and under his sovereignty in the awareness that our place is not of our own winning, but of his own giving.

Sabbath day means cessation from the labor of the daily round of work, the stilling of the whole social structure in recognition of God's ownership and protection. Sabbath rest is an attitude of acknowledgment, a recognition of God's sovereignty over our daily round. It is a trustful reliance on God for meaning and fulfillment of life. The power of the workaday world of money-making and power playing to captivate and dominate us is broken because we know who is master and owner.

The sabbath rest of faith is the rest of surrender to Jesus' lordship. It is a profound recognition that our bodily life is the vehicle of the grace of God and belongs to him. The Sabbath day is the ritual of one rest day in seven. The sabbath rest is an attitude toward our whole physical-psychical beings that releases stress and tension and weariness to God. He is the source of our strength; he is the energizer of our physical life. Sabbath rest calls us to cease our frenzy and open our whole being to the renewing power of God's Spirit.

## • Worship and Praise

Sabbath rest also means worship. The center of the whole Sabbath experience for Israel was the worship of the God who had delivered them from bondage and brought them into covenant relationship with himself in the land of his promise. Sabbath was a day for praise and celebration and covenant renewal. It was a time for remembering who they were and what they were about as the people of God.

All these ideas are gathered together in the sabbath rest of the Christian in the "today" of the gospel era. The rest of the people of God is experienced not only as corporate worship on the Lord's day, but as life centered in God in the posture of worship and praise. Sabbath rest is a life of commitment to God. It is life in a community of faith, devoted to hearing God's voice and obeying it.

Rest is like the keeping of a Sabbath: a center of peace in a world of compulsive activity, a center of security in a world of neurotic self-seeking and manipulation, a center of worship in a world of idolatry and false values. Sabbath rest is the worship and celebration of God. It certainly does not mean the end of action or the end of insecurity or the end of struggle. It does mean life that is God centered and attentive, at rest in his grace.

### ● Rest From Self-Effort

"So then, there remains a sabbath rest for the people of God; for whoever enters God's rest also ceases from his labors as God did from his" (4:9–10). God's own rest from labor is reflected in the Christian pilgrim's release from self-efforts. If we enter by faith we have to give up works, no matter how pious or subtle. We cannot have it both ways. Ceasing from our works means the acceptance of the fact that we cannot earn our peace with God or our standing before him. We are at rest with God by faith in what he has done, "not because of works, lest any man should boast" (Eph. 2:9).

To give up works also means to cease trying to play God and manipulate life. It means giving up our sense of well-being and worth that depends on the multiplication of activities, organizations, and projects. Our labors cannot make us right with God; neither can they satisfy our personal need for a sense of worth and value. There is no rest at the end of our feverish activity and endless works. There is only the demand to do more. We need God's forgiveness for our sins, to be sure, but we also need God's rest from our works!

### ● Hindrances to Sabbath Rest

The author of Hebrews explains some attitudes and behaviors that keep the pilgrim people of God from experiencing the promised rest and continuing to enjoy it. His primary concern appears to be for the condition of the heart. The phrase "do not harden your hearts" is used three times in 3:8–4:10. Other references are "go astray in their hearts" (3:10), "an evil, unbelieving heart" (3:12), and the word of God discerns the "thoughts and intentions of the heart" (4:12).

The heart is the center of both emotions and the will. Just as the heart of a problem involves all aspects of the problem and brings them to a central focus, so the heart of a person involves all aspects of the person and brings them together in a unity of thought and emotion and bodily activity. Participation in the rest that remains means having a heart in right relationship with God; it means the whole person in covenant loyalty to God. A heart that is right with God has the kind of openness and sensitivity to God that keeps the conversation going and is attentive and obedient.

That is why unbelief and lack of confidence are such serious matters. They shift the concern of the heart from God to self and seek to manipulate and control situations that are in the province and providence of God. The fundamental relation of the heart is then with the world and not with God. The core attitude is self-centeredness and anxiety. Life is not lived in faith but in anxious manipulation. That brings a terrible hardness of heart that causes one to "fall away from the living God" (3:12). It leads to a heart that goes "astray," that is, that keeps going unthinkingly off the road, falling into the ditch on one side or the other (3:10). This is a heart deceived by the sin of unbelief. It can no longer be confident; it must be self-protective and callous. The final result can only be a spirit of defensive rebellion against God.

No wonder the exhortations are so intense and the warnings so severe! Great and serious issues are at stake. "Do not harden your hearts" (3:8, 15; 4:7). "Take care, brethren" (3:12). "Let us fear" (4:1). "Let us therefore strive to enter that rest" (4:11). If rest means the end of anxious effort, our striving is surely not an anxiety-filled struggle to be right with God. It is not a subtle form of works righteousness. It is rather, in Robert Jewett's words, "a matter of seeking and holding fast a new relationship that one has been given."

It takes concentration and effort to maintain a good conversation. To maintain the relationship given in grace demands our continual attentiveness. Over and over again the message of Hebrews comes to us: The relationship can be lost, the rest forfeited. Great and gracious promises undergird it, and we are encouraged to press on to make it our own; but the warnings are real and as necessary for us as ever they were for the Hebrews.

## ● Mutual Exhortation

A key exhortation, giving possibility to all the others, is "exhort one another every day, as long as it is called 'today,' that none of you be hardened through the deceitfulness of sin" (3:13). The book of Hebrews is itself an exhortation (13:22) that the writer intends to become the basis of their mutual exhortations every day.

The task of exhortation is not given only to the pastors and teachers and evangelists. The word does not belong to the elite few, the chosen and ordained in-group; it is not sacramentally controlled by the clergy. It is the possession of the body of believers, each member of which is charged with the task of proclamation and sharing. The sermon may speak on Sunday, but every day the members share the word. In that mutual sharing hearts are kept open, dialogue is kept fresh and alive, and we are encouraged to keep on with the pilgrim journey. Every day we are to exhort one another to consider Jesus, to keep the faith, and to endure when the fantastic has faded. This mutual sharing keeps the exhorter and the exhorted on the same level, partakers together of grace and sharers together on the journey.

The substance of the mutual exhortation of believers is the word of God. The word that spoke in creation, incarnation, and redemption is the word that calls the community of faith into being and summons its members into responsive, obedient relationship with God in Christ. It is described as alive and active. It does not fall on our ears and hearts like the "written code" that "kills" (2 Cor. 3:6). It is the word of the living God and is life giving.

The word of God pursues men and women and cries out for personal decision. It is a two-edged sword, discerning and revealing our intentions, making distinctions we could never make by our examination of ourselves. It probes our relation to God and our relation to our own feelings and experiences. There is nothing hidden from the penetration of the living word of God if we are open and vulnerable to him. It is this word that exposes the deceitfulness of sin and keeps the Christian's heart open and responsive to the divinely initiated dialogue. It is this word that we are to share with each other in our mutual exhortations.

Good advices about being happy and getting the most out of life will never save us from sin's deceit. Rules for overcoming inferiority and self-helps for anxiety will never cure our hardness of heart. Only openness to the living, searching, cleansing, and healing word of God can do that (John 17:17).

## ● Conclusion

The "rest of faith" or the "rest that remains" has always been expressive of life in the Spirit. The terms signify a quality of Christian living open to the Christian pilgrim who by faith has trusted the purifying work of Christ to cleanse the heart from its hardness and unbelief and spirit of rebellion. That spirit is the spirit of the carnal mind.

The rest of faith is the rest of a heart that has heard the word of God and responded in openness and obedience. It is a rest that is possible now, in the process of the journey. It is a rest that is promised for the end of the journey to those who persevere in confident hope. Because it is God's rest, it is both present and future; we enter it and experience it, yet must strive to enter it. We never possess it in the sense of ownership. It is God's sabbath rest offered in the "today" of our journey. "Let us therefore strive to enter that rest" (4:11).

## • Discussion Questions

1. How do you respond to the idea that the Christian life is a pilgrimage or a journey? What are some specific ways they can be compared?

2. To the Israelites, Canaan implied rest; they did, in fact, enter Canaan. How, then, could it be said that they did not enter into rest?

3. How would you define "rest" from your reading of Hebrews 3:7–4:13? Is it heaven?

4. I have described the rest of faith as a Sabbath day kind of life. What does this mean? How can we ever find a sabbath rest for our bodies and souls in our hyperactive culture?

5. How can we "cease from our labors" on the one hand, and "strive to enter into rest" on the other?

6. How would you define hardness of heart? This seems very important to the author of Hebrews. Why?

7. What do you think of the idea that we are to exhort one another, not with pious advices and religious clichés, but with the living word of God? How does this idea change our understanding of the way we usually experience going to church and listening to sermons?

8. I understand the sabbath rest that remains for the people of God to be a quality of relationship with God. What are some characteristics of this relationship as seen in Hebrews 3:7–4:13? Can this kind of life be experienced by every Christian? What hinders it? How is this "rest" entered? What are the consequences of not entering?

# CHAPTER · 6

# Jesus Is Our Middleman

Since then we have a great high priest who has passed through the heavens, Jesus, the Son of God, let us hold fast our confession. For we have not a high priest who is unable to sympathize with our weaknesses, but one who in every respect has been tempted as we are, yet without sin. Let us then with confidence draw near to the throne of grace, that we may receive mercy and find grace to help in time of need.

For every high priest chosen from among men is appointed to act on behalf of men in relation to God, to offer gifts and sacrifices for sins. He can deal gently with the ignorant and wayward, since he himself is beset with weakness. Because of this he is bound to offer sacrifice for his own sins as well as for those of his people. And one does not take the honor upon himself, but he is called by God, just as Aaron was. So also Christ did not exalt himself to be made a high priest, but was appointed by him who said to him, "Thou art my Son." . . .

In the days of his flesh, Jesus offered up prayers and supplications, with loud cries and tears, to him who was able to save him from death, and he was heard for his godly fear. Although he was a Son, he learned obedience through what he suffered; and being made perfect he became the source of eternal salvation to all who obey him (Heb. 4:14–5:5, 7–9).

● These verses introduce a central theme of Hebrews, the priesthood of Jesus. It is discussed in great detail in chapters 4–10. In a series of comparisons, analogies, illustrations, and warnings, the writer lifts up Jesus, our priest, and calls us in turn to renewed confidence, faith, and loyalty.

When I think of Jesus, a number of terms, names, and images come to mind. Jesus is Lord; he is Christ; he is Savior. He is Redeemer and King, Shepherd and Friend. The list can grow long. For some reason the term "priest" does not ordinarily come quickly to mind, and I am probably not alone in this. For many Protestant Evangelicals, "priest" is not a common way of thinking about Christ; for some, it is not a congenial one. It is not difficult to understand why.

Old pagan religions had priests. Who has not seen an old TV movie about a South Sea island tribe being destroyed by a terrible drought? The priest chooses the beautiful maiden and sacrifices her to the gods, and the rains come again. Old Testament religion had priests who lived in a strange world of altars and rituals, sacrifices and offerings. But whatever we may think about priests and priesthood, the author of Hebrews portrayed Jesus Christ as our great high priest. He declared Jesus to be the one who alone is able to bring us into right relationship with God and the presence of God.

## ● Both Human and Divine

What do we mean when we say that Jesus is our priest? The role of the priest is to represent God to men and to represent men to God. The priest is the middleman, the mediator who stands between God and men to bring them together. Jesus comes to us from God, all the way into our world to meet us where we are, to act from among us and in our behalf with God. The truth is, we cannot handle our relationship with God by ourselves. We do not have the holiness or the power to come into his presence. Even if we lived blameless lives from this day on, we could never gather up enough merit to compensate for the sins of our yesterdays or heal the estrangement induced by our guilt. There is one who has come among us from God himself who, as one of us, does this very thing for us. It is Jesus our priest.

This section of Hebrews offers a magnificent view of both the divinity and the humanity of Jesus our priest. He is our "great high priest who has passed through the heavens" (4:14). This is the only time in Hebrews that the full title "great high priest" appears. It emphasizes the exalted character of his priesthood and its superiority over that of any other, including Aaron and Melchizedek. Jesus has not merely passed through the veil of the tabernacle that closed off the Holy of Holies, but has "passed through the heavens" into the very presence of God. He has been raised from the dead and exalted at the right hand of the Father and there exercises his priestly role in power and authority.

The author states clearly that our high priest is "Jesus, the Son of God," the incarnate, earthly man who shares the life of the Father and who is one in heart and will with the Father. Whatever it means for Jesus to be our priest, it never means that he is "over against" the Father. He does not seek to placate or cajole the Father into a change of attitude toward us so that he will look upon us with grace instead of judgment. On the contrary, in his priesthood Jesus is in fact being the Father's Son and doing the Father's will in fulfillment of the Father's atoning purpose.

The strong emphasis on the divinity and transcendent authority of our great high priest is matched—almost surpassed—by an emphasis on his humanity and weakness in our behalf. His identification with us in our human frailty is as real and profound as his identification with the Father's divine nature and power. He identifies with us in the weakness of temptation. He is the "one who in every respect has been tempted as we are, yet without sin" (4:5).

In 2:18 a general statement is made about the help Jesus can give the tempted because of his own temptations. Here the reference is more specific. He was tempted "in every respect" and tempted "as we are." The pronoun "we" does not refer, first of all, to us. It reflects the common bond of humanity and the common religious tensions and struggles shared by the writer and the first readers of Hebrews. We know about their temptation to weariness and discouragement. They had left the splendor and status of Jewish religion for the sake of Christ and, in great joy and at great cost, had joined the despised band who followed him. But they were losing the vitality and the fervor of newfound faith and were in danger of pulling back and giving up.

## • With Us in Times of Discouragement and Temptation

The statement that Jesus was tempted "in every respect . . . as we are" recognizes the presence of Jesus in their discouragement and his profound identification with them in their struggle to maintain faith and hope. The temptations of the Hebrews were heightened because they felt they were alone. Thus they were assured that the great high priest was not distant and aloof from them in their time of trial and discouragement. He knew their weaknesses. It is precisely at the point of their weakness that the priest knew them, identified with them, cared for them, and dealt "gently" with them.

Jesus could do this for them because there was no realm of temptation he had not experienced in the same way everyone does. He did not, of course, meet the same specific kinds of temptations that the Hebrews were meeting in their church situation, but the depth of his humanity was such that he could enter totally into their struggles from "inside" and so sustain and strengthen them. (See the discussion of temptation in chapter 3).

It is important to understanding that Jesus' experience of temptation and his sinless victory are not used as an example for us to follow. We are not instructed in the ways to avoid or resist or overcome temptation. What is emphasized is that his deep struggle and strong victory reveal the depth of his ability to empathize and sympathize with us in our weakness. None of us is tempted "in all points," but he was. Limited as we are in both experience and imagination, we cannot share fully in the hurts and burdens and failures even of the ones we know and love the best, but he can. Jesus is able to enter totally into the weakness of our humanity because his entering into our humanity is total. He has become weak and human like us and understands our weakness from inside. He can, then, "deal gently with the ignorant and wayward" (5:2).

There are some who do not know the way or have not really ever heard of the way; others have wandered away. Our priest is able to put himself in the place of those to whom he ministers. His priestly intercession is effective, not because he has been raised above human weaknesses, but precisely because he has entered so fully into them.

I remember conducting a faculty meeting for prayer and sharing. There were the usual requests about the sick, about the pressures students were experiencing, and the like. The whole atmosphere was transformed when one of our colleagues expressed the way Christ had been real to her as she had made her urgent, fearful search for her biological father. Her openness and vulnerability were a powerful witness to the life of Jesus at work in her—and suddenly, at work in us all in new ways. Our polite, protective prayer requests were no longer valid. We had to be open and real before God and each other because someone shared with us from "inside." That is the way our priest comes to us.

## ● With Us in Our Suffering and Dying

Jesus our priest also identifies with us in the weakness of our suffering and dying. Our human condition is temptation and sin; it is also weakness, suffering, and death. Jesus knows the anguish of our mortality. "In the days of his flesh, Jesus offered up prayers and supplications, with loud cries and tears, to him who was able to save him from death" (5:7).

Our minds are drawn to Jesus' agony in the garden of Gethsemane where, with soul "sorrowful, even to death," he prayed, "Abba, Father, all things are possible to thee; remove this cup from me; yet not what I will, but what thou wilt" (Mark 14:34, 36). Out of the depths he cried to his Father to be delivered from death. He was not, in fact, delivered, but went on to die in the desolation of the cross. All his holy life and obedience did not bring him "joy without sorrow, peace without pain"; nor did his prayerful agony save him from the sense of alienation and separation from God. Yet he was heard! The relationship that he no longer felt was nevertheless real. The abandonment he experienced did not mean that the Father had abandoned him.

Jesus never broke the dialogue with his Father even in his deepest suffering. He cried out *to* his Father and was heard. The conversation was not broken, and neither was the relationship. Sonship and suffering are not mutually exclusive. It is as the Son of God that Jesus cries out of his despair to his Father, and it is as Son that he is heard by the Father.

This reference to the depths of Jesus' agony and cry to the one who could save him from death must imply that the Hebrews themselves were in real and deep distress. The very meaning of their lives was at stake in their commitment to Christ. They saw in him the fulfillment of their long history as God's people. They understood his as the completion of their ancient laws and prophecies, rituals and traditions. Everything was at stake in the authenticity and the truthfulness of Jesus.

When the Hebrews began to doubt and pull away and lose heart concerning these great realities, they put themselves in a situation as dark and deep as death itself. They desperately needed to know that their high priest knew the pangs of death and that he would deal with them deeply and gently. Out of the depths he had cried—and was heard. Out of the depths they, too, were crying— and were heard. And out of the depths we cry—and are heard by the one who can save us. "Yea, though I walk through the valley of the shadow of death, I will fear no evil: for thou art with me" (Ps. 23:4 KJV).

Through the agony of his suffering Jesus learned obedience; that is, he came to ever deeper experiences of obedience. He did not need to learn obedience over against disobedience. He did not suffer because he was disobedient and needed to learn to obey. Rather, in the words of F. F. Bruce, "he learned by his experience of suffering what obedience to God involved in man's life on earth." His deep, personal experience of suffering made him "perfect," or perfectly qualified to "become the source of eternal salvation to all who obey him" (5:9). Here again the emphasis is not on the weakness and pain and suffering of Jesus as such; the whole point is that he is able both to identify with us in our most profound human weaknesses and to provide full salvation for us through his participation in our humanity.

## • "The Man of God's Own Choosing"

I think it is very significant that in this section of Hebrews there is a genuine and total acceptance of the reality of human weakness and vulnerability to temptation, waywardness, suffering, and death. None of these is denied and none is condemned. They are all taken for granted and are indeed the base reality behind the very existence and purpose of the priesthood. Our humanity is not denied or rejected; rather, a priest is provided to deal with it. We are released from the futile struggle to overcome our faults and failures in order to come into God's presence. Our great high priest has come into our faulting, failing humanity to bring us, just as we are, into the reconciling, purifying presence of God.

In his humility our priest "does not take the honor upon himself, but he is called by God" (5:4). He does not offer sacrifice for his own sins (5:3) because, though tempted, he is "without sin" (4:15). But he does not presume upon his divine nature or his regal status. We are reminded of the hymn of Christ's self-emptying in Paul's letter to the Philippians. Jesus "did not count equality with God a thing to be grasped, but emptied himself, taking the form of a servant, being born in the likeness of men. And being found in human form he humbled himself and became obedient unto death, even death on a cross" (2:6–8).

Christ is one with the Father and obedient to the Father in his high priestly role. It is the willing God who seeks to bring unwilling men into his holy fellowship. It is God who provides the means by which sinful humanity can be restored to right relationship with himself. The offended one himself provides for the removal of the offense; the sinned-against provides the sinner with the means of forgiveness. God opens up the way back to him by himself becoming, in Jesus, the way (John 14:6).

Can we see how this reverses our ordinary way of thinking about our relationship to God?

It is one thing to come to God with whatever gifts or obedience we can manage and offer them for the purpose of finding acceptance or favor from him. It is one thing to come to God in contrition and remorse to deplore ourselves in his presence and beg for forgiveness. It is one thing for us to select a special person from among ourselves and dedicate this one to sacrifice what is precious and intercede before God for mercy on our behalf.

It is something else, something wonderful, if God *himself* takes the initiative and comes to us in our guilt and alienation and offers, in Jesus, an obedience we could never achieve. It is something else, something marvelous, if God *himself* comes in Jesus to identify with us completely in our sinful humanity and, in our behalf, to be the sacrifice for our sins against him. Our sacrificing, interceding priest is not one of our choosing; he is one of our own, "the man of God's own choosing." God provides the means of our otherwise impossible approach to him!

● "Hold Fast Our Confession"

The two exhortations of this section take on special meaning when seen in this context. The first one is in 4:14: "Let us hold fast our confession." In 3:1, Jesus, our apostle and high priest, is the one we confess, the one we own as giving identity and meaning to our lives. In 11:13 the patriarchs, having seen and embraced the promise of God, confessed "that they were strangers and exiles on the earth." Their confession identified them as people whose native land was elsewhere. Their existence was not defined for them by their world, but by their God, who had called them to another citizenship.

Thus the confession we hold fast is not a confession of sin or weakness, nor is it a confession of a creed or a doctrine. It is the confession of Christ by whom our lives are defined. The meaning of our existence is not defined by our world and its values, but by Christ. Our confession of him both identifies us with him and commits us to him.

"Hold fast" is a forceful word that comes from the word for power. To "hold fast our confession" is to make the declaration that identifies us with Jesus our sovereign and suffering high priest; it is to make it boldly and to hold on to it in the face of all odds. The exhortation is in the present tense, indicating continued or repeated action. So we are to continue to keep a firm grasp on our confession day by day. The recognition of our human weakness makes the exhortation all the more urgent. We are vulnerable to discouragement and weariness, to loss of vision and nerve. The answer is not to lose hope or give up, but to trust the sustaining presence of our priest and make our daily confession of him.

## • "Draw Near to the Throne of Grace"

The other exhortation is in 4:16: "Let us then with confidence draw near to the throne of grace, that we may receive mercy and find grace to help in time of need." Drawing near or approaching God is the great point of Hebrews. We have a better hope (than Melchizedek or the law could give us) "through which we draw near to God" (7:19). Since Jesus lives to make intercession for us, "he is able for all time to save those who draw near to God through him" (7:25). The law cannot "make perfect those who draw near," but through the blood of Jesus, our great priest, we may "draw near with a true heart in full assurance of faith" (10:1, 22).

We are encouraged to come to the "throne," that is, the very presence of God, the sovereign ruler. We can come only because it is a throne of grace. The symbol of power is defined in terms of grace and mercy. We come to God, the merciful ruler. The

Hebrews did not have courage enough to come to God; they thought that they did not have power enough and that as long as they were weak, there was no hope. They are not alone. "I can't." "I am not strong enough to make it." "How could I be accepted?"

Not enough courage, not enough power: that's our situation. Our great high priest contradicts these false ideas and comes to us in weakness. He shares our mortality, letting us know that just as we are, fully human, we may approach the throne. It is a throne of grace. There is no hierarchy of grace. Jesus has opened the way for us all.

## • Conclusion

The whole business of a priest is to bring God and man together. Under the old system it could never really happen because the priest, himself human and sinful, was always in between. The priest who was meant to bring God and the people together was also the very one who kept them separate. The whole system that was intended to bring them together stood in between and was actually in the way.

But if the one in the middle is really God himself in Jesus, if the middleman is also really one of us, then he who stands as our mediator does not divide. It is precisely in him, the God-man, that we are brought together.

I talked to a student who was sick in body and in spirit. She hated herself and felt that no one loved her. Many tried to love her, but she wouldn't believe and couldn't believe. She could not handle her emotions and could not cope. I said to her, "You really do need a priest; someone who understands you, who totally knows and feels where you are, who is with you, who is on your side, and can take your case all the way to God! Jesus is your priest." We all really do need a priest!

The glory of the gospel is that in Jesus, God is not out there waiting to be "come to"; in Jesus he has come! To give our case to Jesus, the man among us, is in fact to give it to God. Some of us feel the stress of working and coping and making it. Some of us are struggling with temptation and guilt or broken relationships. We have experienced sickness and sorrow and death. Do you know what we need? We need a priest. We need a priest because we are weak and cannot take our own case all the way. We need someone to be with us where we are who is also where God is. We cannot make it without God. We need someone who totally understands us to bear with us and to empathize with the reality of our needs. Jesus is right there. Right here!

There are some for whom God is far away. For all the gospel that has been heard, he is not yet near and personal. The consciousness of sin and uncleanliness still dominates attempts to pray or to worship or to live right. The word of the gospel is that Jesus brings God to us. He is our priest who brings us to God. He is the one to whom we may confess our sins. He can come to where we are and take our case all the way to the Father. We really do have a priest!

## ● Discussion Questions

1. What words or phrases come to your mind as you think of the person and work of Jesus? Is "priest" normally on your list? Would you agree that for many Protestant Evangelicals the idea of priesthood is not especially appealing? Why or why not?

2. Why is it so important that Jesus be divine in order to be our priest? Why is it emphasized so much in Hebrews that Jesus must be human to be our priest?

3. I have emphasized the reality of the weakness, temptations, and vulnerability of Jesus as our high priest. What is your response to this idea? Why do we often fail to identify with the concept of a priest?

4. Discuss the idea that the temptations of Jesus are not used to give us help in overcoming our own temptations, but rather to reveal the depth of his identification with us in our weakness and susceptibility to temptation.

5. Jesus was not spared from death when he cried out to the one who could save him from death. But he continued his dialogue with God

and was heard by God. In what ways is this important for us for understanding our life and suffering as Christians?

6. What do you think is meant by the statement that Jesus learned obedience by what he suffered? How does that make him perfect?

7. I believe it is hard for us to come to God as we are in our humanness, because we think we must overcome both our sin and our humanity. What do you think?

8. Discuss how the fact that God himself provides the way for sinful humanity to come to him changes our usual understanding of our approach to him. We want him to change his attitude toward us and not condemn us. He wants us to change our attitude toward him and come as we are. What do you think about this?

# CHAPTER · 7

# A Call to Maturity

About this we have much to say which is hard to explain, since you have become dull of hearing. For though by this time you ought to be teachers you need some one to teach you again the first principles of God's word. You need milk, not solid food; for every one who lives on milk is unskilled in the word of righteousness, for he is a child. But solid food is for the mature, for those who have their faculties trained by practice to distinguish good from evil.

Therefore let us leave the elementary doctrine of Christ and go on to maturity, not laying again a foundation of repentance from dead works and of faith toward God, with instruction about ablutions, the laying on of hands, the resurrection of the dead, and eternal judgment. And this we will do if God permits. For it is impossible to restore again to repentance those who have once been enlightened, who have tasted the heavenly gift, and have become partakers of the Holy Spirit, and have tasted the goodness of the word of God and the powers of the age to come, if they then commit apostasy, since they crucify the Son of God on their own account and hold him up to contempt. . . .

Though we speak thus, yet in your case, beloved, we feel sure of better things that belong to salvation. . . . And we desire each one of you to show the same earnestness in realizing the full assurance of hope until the end, so that you may not be sluggish, but imitators of those who through faith and patience inherit the promises (Heb. 5:11–6:6; 6:9, 11–12).

● I heard Bob Benson say, "I'm still trying to find out what I want to be when I grow up!" That's my testimony, too. After more than sixty years of living I am still trying to grow up—and am way behind in the process. I do not feel alone in this, however. Most of us have a lot of maturing to do. I believe there is help for us in the exhortations and warnings of this passage of Scripture.

In the verse preceding this passage, the author concluded that Christ was designated a high priest after the order of Melchizedek (5:10). One would expect the discussion to continue with some explanation of the priesthood of this person and its relation to Christ. But it doesn't. Instead, the writer breaks his train of thought to confront the Hebrews with a problem they have created for him. There is much more he would like to say about the priesthood of Christ, but because they have become "dull of hearing," it is hard to explain. They need what he has to tell them and should be well able to understand and respond. They have, in fact, been believers long enough to know enough to teach others, but they have regressed to the point where they need someone to teach them again the ABC's of God's word. They are children, not adults, and need milk when they should be eating solid food.

These verses place a striking emphasis on the word and on hearing. In 5:11 it is said that the Hebrews' hearing is dull. They need teachers to teach them God's word (5:12). They are to leave the elementary doctrine (word) of Christ and go on to maturity (6:1). They have tasted the goodness of the word of God (6:5) but are still in danger of committing apostasy.

There is much more involved in the word than true doctrine or teaching. There is more in it than intellectual content and more is demanded than intellectual understanding. The word of God confronts us and calls us into a personal relationship with him that involves the whole of life. The word of God calls us into covenant partnership with God and with one another. It is a relationship intended to be dynamic and growing, leading to personal maturity.

## • Drifting in Apathy

The Hebrews were immature because they had fallen into habitual apathy toward the truth of God. Their condition was the result of laziness rather than ignorance. Sluggish—not low—intelligence was their problem. They were not really listening, not really hearing, in the sense of attentively responding to the word of God. Their tragedy was their regression.

They had not always been dull of hearing. Time was when they lived in the light and suffered for Christ with joy (10:32–34). They should be continuing their glad journey, growing and learning and teaching, developing in ethical discernment and spiritual insight. But they were not paying attention to what they had heard and were drifting away (2:1). They had developed beyond first principles years ago, but they quit thinking about new things and hard things, so were back where they started—and in danger of losing it all.

Thomas Hewitt put it, "If dark things do not become plain, then plain things will become dark." Jesus said, "For to him who has will more be given; and he will have in abundance, but from him who has not, even what he has will be taken away" (Matt. 13:12). We can feel the deep concern of the author-pastor for the Hebrews. His pastoral exhortations and warnings were intense because their situation was desperate.

We can well imagine what his concern for us would be. How like them we are! Too many of us are shallow and immature. We have developed our own habits of spiritual apathy toward the things of God. We do not want to think about things that demand concentration or that force us to make personal decisions. We are content to know what we know and listen to sermons that tell us what we already believe. Like the Hebrews, our problem is not our ignorance, but our dullness of hearing. We seldom search the Bible or work with a concordance or talk seriously with a friend to understand better and to incorporate into our lives the truths we claim to live by.

I deliberately do not use the phrase "find the answers." We are great at finding answers. "How-to" books abound, as do Bible study groups and conferences and seminars. Authoritative religious leaders give us laws to memorize, rules to learn, and principles to follow for understanding the Bible, being filled with the Spirit, witnessing, raising our family and reaching our potential for health and wealth. But what do we have that is really our own?

A minister-friend's children gave him a red book, beautifully bound, filled with blank pages. It is the book of his own theology. He writes in it from time to time the things he has come to know and believe about his Christian faith. It is not a book that is easy to write; it is not a book for others to read. But it is a wonderful book because it is his effort to articulate his own faith as he lives out and thinks out his response to the word that has encountered him in Jesus.

Is there anything we are working on, thinking about, and struggling with that we seek to appropriate for our lives? Our intellectual lethargy can coexist with all kinds of religious "answer-finding" activities. The tragedy is that our hunger for answers makes us highly susceptible to just about any teaching that comes along, especially if the teacher is articulate, simplistic, and absolutistic and has charisma.

The maturity for which the writer-pastor of Hebrews pleads is not of this sort. It is instead a personal maturity that comes from responding attentively to the word that has been spoken in Jesus. As we respond with our whole selves—body, soul and spirit—we are brought into a living relationship with God.

The maturity of that relationship is expressed through discerning ethical choices. The mature are "those who have their faculties trained by practice to distinguish good from evil" (5:14). By constant use they "have trained themselves to distinguish good from evil" (NIV). "Faculties" is a word that refers to the ability to make moral decisions. It is not the word for intellectual perception. The "mature" are not characterized by their understanding of doctrine or spiritual truth. Nor are they those who have the assumed "spiritual" maturity that comes from years of familiarity with the words and ways of the church. They are those who attentively participate in conversation with God our covenant partner and in deliberate obedience seek to make right moral and ethical choices.

## ● Discerning Right From Wrong

The development of ethical discernment, the ability to know and do right from wrong, does not come automatically with the new birth. Neither does it come with the fullness of the Holy Spirit. Great spiritual experiences do not produce it. It is the result of care and discipline and practice. The writer uses the language of athletic training.

A very significant issue is raised here: Where do we learn what is right and what is wrong? Where are we getting our signals for the choices and decisions we make day by day? If our attention is not toward the word of God—I do not mean just the Bible, but the word as spoken to us in Jesus, his life and teachings and his "mind" (Phil. 2:1–11)—then we are learning values from whatever pressures are strongest at the time of decision. Or we fall back into whatever old ways of reacting and deciding have become habitual with us.

The phrase "trained by practice to distinguish good from evil" (5:14) is a realistic and helpful one because the Hebrews would not get "answers" even from the Word of God. So it is with us. Seldom is there a one-to-one relationship between the issue we must decide and a verse from the Bible. To paraphrase F. F. Bruce, our maturity comes as we truly appropriate the essence of the gospel in our hearts and learn to regulate our lives by it. This process of internalizing is long and difficult and cannot be shortcut by memorizing verses or rules or guiding principles. As much as these may help, we must learn for ourselves by practice to distinguish good from evil. The choices must come from within us as we mature in our response to the word of God and grow in him on the journey.

We would expect that the writer-pastor, having demonstrated that the Hebrews were not ready for meat, would give them the milk they needed. Instead, he identifies with them in a twofold exhortation: "Let us leave . . . and go on" (6:1). And one is as important as the other. The goal is maturity, a word also translated "perfection" or "full growth." In light of the reference to childhood, "full adulthood" may be a good way to express it.

The phrase "go on to maturity" is literally translated "let us be borne on to maturity." There is a strong emphasis in Hebrews on personal responsibility and response to the divine initiative. We do not present to God a mature specimen of our own creation. We are "borne along" as we respond to the one who "is at work in [us], both to will and to work for his good pleasure" (Phil. 2:13).

## ● Building on the Foundation

The process of maturity means leaving behind the "elementary doctrine of Christ" and not rebuilding foundations. Three pairs of elementary doctrines are mentioned. They are of special interest because they indicate an early process of doctrinal formulation in the young Christian church. These teachings were probably used in catechism classes or taught to young converts. They are representative of early basic Christian doctrine.

The first pair are called the foundation: repentance from dead works and faith toward God. The ministries of John the Baptist and Jesus began with the call to repentance. It means not just sorrow for the guilt of sin, but a change of mind and direction. To leave the pagan, gentile world or the religious Jewish world and join the Christian movement involved more than emotional experience; it demanded a radical change of direction and perspective. Old works led to death; repentance and faith in God lead one to join the pilgrim people on their journey to life.

The next two pairs of terms are called "instructions." "Ablutions" or "baptisms" or "washings" would be a subject of instruction for young converts. The baptism of John, the washings in Jewish ritual and especially in sects such as the Qumran community, and the baptisms of the contemporary pagan religions would surely call for some clarification of the relation of these to Christian baptism. The latter always symbolized entrance into the Christian faith. In the early church, the laying on of hands was connected with healing and with receiving the Holy Spirit. Resurrection and judgment were themes prominent in the earliest preaching of the apostles. Christians lived by the Spirit in the power of the resurrection of Christ and looked toward and hoped for the final resurrection and the judgment—the consummation and triumph of God's purposes.

Some questions are unavoidable: Why should such fundamental teachings be left behind in order to progress toward maturity? In what sense are they left behind? Surely the writer is not saying that once you go beyond fundamentals they are no longer important. Perhaps the idea is not so much that foundational elements be left behind as that they not be continually repeated, "not laying again a foundation."

T. H. Robinson, in the *Moffatt New Testament Commentary,* makes the observation that we can never make progress unless we are prepared to "accept the validity" of our experience and to "assume the stability" of our original position. This is the very point made in Hebrews. We cannot go forward if we are continually reproving our basic positions. How many times are the foundations to be laid? Their whole purpose is to provide the base for building. Robinson says that "the refusal to accept them and to build upon them is the direct opposite of faith."

To build on the foundation is not to forget. Astronomers do not re-prove the laws of gravity; they "forget" them in their constant use of them as they go on to do their real work. The biographer does not redo the alphabet; it is both continually used and totally forgotten in the process of character analysis.

The same is true for the Christian. Let us take repentance as an example. Repentance is fundamental to conversion to Christianity. It means a basic, radical turnaround, a "U turn" of the mind and heart and will from self and sin to following after God. The maturing Christian does not go back to that basic turnaround over and over again. At the same time, repentance is a continuing reality in the life of the Christian. Shortcomings and failures of whatever sort—indeed, our very humanity with its weaknesses— call for repentance in every child of God, however saintly. But the foundation of repentance is not laid again and again. It is "forgotten" in the life of repentant openness and obedience to the Spirit of God. It is an "elementary doctrine" that is left behind in the progress and joy of our faith.

Some scholars say that the points of "elementary doctrine" included elements from first-century Judaism and contemporary pagan religious practices. The coming of Christ and his priesthood, death, and resurrection gave old Jewish practices and rituals a new and living meaning. Now the Hebrews were looking back to old beliefs and old customs, questioning again the issues they had once settled. The "elementary doctrines" had ceased to be living expressions of a personal relationship with Christ and had become simply doctrinal or ritual matters more or less congenial with those found within Judaism. The Hebrews were turning away from lively participation in dialogue with their covenant partner and were in terrible danger of losing their faith and life in Christ.

The answer is not "back there." Maturity is up ahead on the pilgrim journey. The writer is optimistic that the Hebrews will join him on the way as they find their strength in God. "And this we will do if God permits" (6:3). This is not an equivalent of our casual remark "Lord willing." It is a serious line and fits with the word "being borne on" toward maturity in 6:1. Certainly it is God's will that we move on in relationship with him. The phrase, however, puts God at the center and not ourselves. Going on is not automatic; it happens under God's conditions. We can neither originate nor manipulate the relationship. We assume we can come and go in and out of faith, in and out of obedience, in and out of grace at our own discretion. We assume grace is always there for the asking; "Jesus paid it all," and there is forgiveness anytime we want. No! It is of God's permission, not our own.

## • A Warning Against Apostasy

"For it is impossible to restore again to repentance those who have once been enlightened, who have tasted the heavenly gift, and have become partakers of the Holy Spirit, and have tasted the goodness of the word of God and the powers of the age to come, if they then commit apostasy, since they crucify the Son of God on their own account and hold him up to contempt" (6:4–6). These awe-filled words reveal the dark, negative side of the requirement to go on to maturity in our life with God. No one can restore the person who turns away from the salvation offered by God in Christ. We are tempted to rephrase or redefine the words to make them less radical and give them a more congenial tone.

Perhaps a brief word of definition would be helpful. The "unforgivable sin" in this passage is apostasy, that is, turning away from Christ as God's means of salvation. It is one thing to sin or fail or backslide, serious as these things are; it is another, having known Christ and his salvation, to deliberately reject and deny him.

The great terms used to describe the divine realities of grace into which the Hebrews had entered only make the possibility of apostasy more appalling: "enlightened," "tasted the heavenly gift," "partakers of the Holy Spirit," "tasted the good things of the word of God and the powers of the world to come." These are not just blessings, but also the realities of the new age inaugurated by the coming of Messiah; they are the saving gifts of Christ. God's salvation has come to the Hebrews not as teaching or doctrine or idea, but as life and power. If they turn their backs on this very life, what is left? If Christ as God's salvation is rejected, where is salvation? If they turn from the living God, where is life to be found? If the heart of the gospel is a matter of doctrinal truth or creedal precision or right belief, it can be discussed, edited, considered, and reflected upon. But if it is life—the alternative is death.

The situation is hypothetical. The writer is sure that he is not describing the circumstances of his readers; theirs are "better things that belong to salvation" (6:9). But the warning is real, and the results of apostasy are awful. The word of 2:3 is heard again: "How shall we escape if we neglect such a great salvation?"

## • The Means to Maturity

Well, what are we to do? Building again the foundation and starting over is evidently not the way. We certainly cannot afford to turn back! The call to all of us "milk-fed" children is to go forward to maturity.

Surely there is a wonderful formula, a marvelous word, to make us mature. Yes, there are in fact three words. They are the great, new, life-changing, miracle-working, maturity-producing words. They are the small, ordinary, old, common maturity-producing words. They are "hope" and "faith" and "patience."

The Hebrews had begun their journey by setting their hope on Jesus, but now it was lagging. They needed to look to him again, put their whole trust in him again, and be renewed. That is another way of saying "faith." By faith the Hebrews had grasped the promises of God and had embraced them and made their confession. By faith they now were to hold on to the promises, their commitment, and the relationship inaugurated by the word of God. That is another way of saying "patient endurance."

The author's urgent call to maturity is not followed by any magic "how-to's," no neat formulas, no shortcut methods. Those who have gone before us made it because they didn't quit. They matured because they held on to the promises, didn't let go of the Promisor, and kept on going. When all is said and done, that is the way to maturity. We all begin the journey with hope and faith. We continue it, from here to maturity, with hope and faith and patience—just like all the other saints who ever lived.

## • Discussion Questions

1. This chapter is on Christian maturity, yet it is a very hard word to define. How would you describe a "mature" Christian?
2. We all struggle with the problem of dull or slow hearing. Discuss the idea that God calls us to conversation or dialogue and we are to listen with our whole selves and respond in a lively way. What makes us dull of hearing? What can we do about it?

3. I have suggested that inattentiveness to God's word (not only the Bible) and our failure to appropriate it is one of the great dangers we face in the Christian church today. What do you think? What can we do about it?

4. Do you agree that the new birth and the fullness of the Holy Spirit do not produce ethical discernment? How would you describe the road to ethical maturity? What are some practical helps we need along the way?

5. Describe someone in your experience who is really mature in Christ. In what ways is that person different from a new believer? What characteristics have not changed in that person's life through the years?

6. What is your personal response to Hebrews 6:4–6? If the writer does not think his readers will commit apostasy, what does he mean and why is the warning so strong?

7. In relation to Hebrews 6:4–6, do you think the distinction I have made between backsliding and apostasy is valid or helpful? Explain your answer.

8. I have said that when it comes right down to it, the good word on how to mature is the same old word of hope and faith and patience. How do you respond to this? Is maturity actually just a matter of being a Christian a long time?

# CHAPTER · 8

# Jesus Our Priest Forever

Now if perfection had been attainable through the Levitical priesthood (for under it the people received the law), what further need would there have been for another priest to arise after the order of Melchizedek, rather than one named after the order of Aaron? For when there is a change in the priesthood, there is necessarily a change in the law as well. For the one of whom these things are spoken belonged to another tribe, from which no one has ever served at the altar. For it is evident that our Lord was descended from Judah, and in connection with that tribe Moses said nothing about priests.

This becomes even more evident when another priest arises in the likeness of Melchizedek, who has become a priest, not according to a legal requirement concerning bodily descent but by the power of an indestructible life. For it is witnessed of him,

> "Thou art a priest for ever,
> after the order of Melchizedek."

On the one hand, a former commandment is set aside because of its weakness and uselessness (for the law made nothing perfect); on the other hand, a better hope is introduced, through which we draw near to God. . . .

The former priests were many in number, because they were prevented by death from continuing in office; but he holds his priesthood permanently, because he continues for ever. Consequently he is able for all time to save those who draw near to God through him, since he always lives to make intercession for them (Heb. 7:11–19, 23–25).

● Our high priest, we are told, is much like a remarkable priest named Melchizedek. That may not be exciting information, but it lies at the heart of the teaching of Hebrews about Jesus our priest. Our quest in this chapter is to find out why.

We have learned so far that Jesus was made like us and so is able to be merciful and faithful (2:17–18). He has come into the very presence of God. He gives his people confidence to draw near to the source of grace (4:14–16). He is a priest who continues forever, "after the order of Melchizedek" (5:1–10).

Instead of explaining right away about Melchizedek, however, the writer digresses to warn and exhort his readers about their immaturity and dullness of hearing and the terrible danger of losing their faith. He is ready now, having laid before them God's promise and his oath as ground for their confidence (6:13–20), to proceed with his discussion of the high priesthood of Christ after the order of Melchizedek.

## ● A Different Kind of Priest

The writer begins with Abraham. As he was returning from his victorious battle with the kings who had overcome Sodom and taken Lot and his family captive, Abraham was met by a priest-king named Melchizedek. "And Melchizedek king of Salem brought out bread and wine; he was priest of God Most High [El Elyon]. And he blessed him and said, 'Blessed be Abram by God Most High, maker of heaven and earth; and blessed be God Most High, who has delivered your enemies into your hand!' And Abram gave him a tenth of everything" (Gen. 14:18–20).

That's the whole story of Melchizedek. Nothing more is said of this mysterious person for a thousand years. Then, in a messianic psalm of King David's time (quoted by Jesus in reference to himself in Mark 12:26, and by Peter in reference to Jesus in Acts 2:34), the statement is made, "You are a priest for ever after the order of Melchizedek" (Ps. 110:4). Nothing more is said for another thousand years. Then the writer of Hebrews brings together the Genesis story and the messianic psalm to proclaim the supreme and revolutionary character of the high priesthood of Jesus.

For most of us, our understanding and appreciation of Jesus our priest are little enhanced by thoughts of Melchizedek! Not so for the concerned pastor-author of Hebrews. Melchizedek is as significant for his understanding of the forgiveness of sin as Abraham is for Paul's understanding of justification by faith. Let's characterize this mysterious priestly figure and then try to understand how he relates to the priesthood of Jesus.

Melchizedek was king of Salem and a priest of the most high God. Abraham, the patriarch of the Israelites, bowed to his blessing and gave to him the tithe of all his booty. And that's the whole story!

It seems that what is *not* said about Melchizedek is as significant as what is. For example, nothing is said of the things that guarantee authenticity to a priest's ministry. No word is given about his ancestry, his birth, his death, or his descendants. He appears as from nowhere, acts as priest to Abraham, and then disappears. He is without genealogy, without progeny, and without system. Yet he has authority to bless the very one through whom Israel receives its genealogy, law, priesthood, and system. Melchizedek therefore bears witness to a valid and superior order of priesthood, prior to and outside the priestly order of Aaron and Levi descending from Abraham. And this is the point: The priesthood of Jesus is the Melchizedek type and not the Aaron-Levi type.

I perceive that the author of Hebrews understood some things very well. For one thing, he understood the origin and history of the priesthood in Israel. He knew its practices and procedures, its rituals and its traditions, and its intentions and purposes. The priest made expiation, or atonement, for the sins of the people (2:17); in this deed he showed himself sympathetic to their weaknesses (4:15). The priest acted in behalf of people in relation to God to offer gifts and sacrifices for sin (5:1) and to offer intercession for them (7:25).

## ● Assurance at Last

There was something else the author understood all too well. The priestly system, for all its divine origin, tradition, and grandeur, never quite succeeded in fulfilling its purposes. Because priests died and were succeeded by others, their intercession could not be continual (7:25). Moreover, the hunger of the worshiper for the cleansing of conscience was never really satisfied; the repeated offerings of blood sacrifice could never actually take sin away (10:1–4). Thus those who came to God could not come into his presence with the confidence of sins really forgiven.

The author's language in his discussion of the failure of the Levitical priesthood is not the language of personal testimony. When Paul writes of the failure of the law, as in Romans 7, we read of his personal struggle and can identify with him in his failures. We wish the writer of Hebrews had been as confessional. However, the seriousness and intensity of his teaching make us think that he deeply felt the failure of his own religious heritage to bring forgiveness of sins and confidence before God. He doesn't speak of himself, but it is not hard to believe that he was giving his own testimony. His years of participation in the sacrificial system had never brought him to full assurance of faith.

That sounds familiar, doesn't it? I talked with a man who had participated for years in the religious life of his church with a hungry heart. And then, through a clear word of love and concern from a friend, his heart opened to Christ and he was filled with confidence and joy in the Lord. That's what happened to the writer of Hebrews. One day some of "those who heard" the Lord bore their witness to the congregation of which he was a part. Their testimony of Jesus, God's son and final self-revelation, was validated by the miraculous ministry of the Holy Spirit (2:3–4), and he was won to Christ forever.

He heard the word, gave close attention, opened his heart to Christ, and experienced the full reality of all that the old system promised but could never provide. He responded to the word of God incarnate in Christ and entered into dialogue with God. Jesus

Christ filled his whole horizon—Christ the eternal Son and final revelation of God. The writer came to know him as the one whom God "appointed the heir of all things, through whom also he created the world," . . . who "reflects the glory of God and bears the very stamp of his nature, upholding the universe by his word of power," . . . who "when he had made purification for sins, . . . sat down at the right hand of the Majesty on high" with a name above all names (1:1–3).

I believe this person suffered most from an awareness of personal impurity and a sense of estrangement from God. That is why he emphasizes so much the priesthood of Jesus, who came from God all the way into our fallen humanity and offered himself as the sacrifice for our sins and opened up the way for us to come, forgiven and cleansed, into the presence of God. He knew Christ as the one "made like his brethren in every respect, so that he might become a merciful and faithful high priest in the service of God, to make expiation for the sins of the people" (2:17). "He is able for all time to save those who draw near to God through him, since he always lives to make intercession for them" (7:25). Sinless, he offered himself "once for all" for the sins of the people (7:27). He is our great high priest who accomplishes in fact and reality the salvation symbolized by the tabernacle, offerings, and sacrifices presided over by the priests in the lineage of Levi. In himself and his self-offering to his father, Jesus makes possible real forgiveness and cleansing from sin and opens the way to right relationship with God.

The awareness of personal sin and uncleanliness, and the feeling of distance from God—I think I have met these two experiences more than any others as I have counseled with students. For years Nancy could tell others of the unconditional love and forgiveness of God, but could never believe them for herself. Not until someone, over a long period of time, kept on loving and caring for her in spite of herself did she come to really trust the One who was all along by her side, on her side, bringing her to God.

Nancy found, as did the Hebrew writer, that Jesus is the one who in himself and his work totally fulfills the ministry of a priest.

## ● Connecting Old and New

But there is a problem. This priest did not come from the tribe of Levi, nor did he in any way share in the appointed line of the Old Testament priesthood. He "belonged to another tribe, from which no one has ever served at the altar ... Judah, and in connection with that tribe Moses said nothing about priests" (7:13–14). Jesus had no priestly genealogy, no priestly credentials, and came from no priestly system. Yet he is a priest who has a better name and offers a better sacrifice, a better intercession, and a better hope because he offers a real and permanent salvation.

This is where Melchizedek fits into the original, radical thinking of the writer to the Hebrews. Melchizedek was a priest before Abraham's descendants established the priesthood. He did not come within the priestly system of Aaron-Levi; he was prior to them and therefore superior to them. He had no genealogy, no progeny, and no system, yet he blessed Abraham and, as an inferior to a superior, Abraham paid tithes to him (7:4–10). Therefore the writer to the Hebrews validates the priesthood of Jesus by connecting it not with Aaron and Levi, but with Melchizedek.

Through this connection, the entire priestly order and the whole sacrificial system of Judaism are declared to be fulfilled and transcended in Jesus Christ. They are pronounced obsolete and so are set aside. In setting aside the sacrificial system, the Mosaic law is also set aside, for it was through the law that the sacrificial system was established (7:12, 18). The whole Levitical system is challenged—in fact, declared invalid along with the legal system that sustained it. Jesus Christ is the eternal priest who has made the perfect sacrifice and oblation for all the sins of all mankind for all time. He is the one who fulfills all the unfulfilled promises for full release from sin, full cleansing from its pollution, and full confidence before God.

William Manson, in his exposition *The Epistle to the Hebrews,* draws a comparison between the way Hebrews deals with the priesthood and the way Paul deals with the law (Rom. 4; Gal. 3).

Paul saw that the promise to Abraham preceded the law; therefore the law could not invalidate the promise. The writer to the Hebrews saw that Melchizedek preceded the Levitical code; therefore the priestly order of Melchizedek could not be cancelled by the Levitical priesthood. Paul's experience with sin and law revealed that the law could never bring him into right relationship with God. The experience of the author of Hebrews with sin and the sacrificial system revealed that sacrifice could never bring him forgiveness of sins. For Paul, Christ is the end of the law and so also the end of the priesthood. In Hebrews, Christ is the end of the priesthood and therefore the end of the law that created it.

In each case the coming of Christ brought a new order, a new way, a new approach to God that at the same time fulfilled the old and transcended it. "Therefore, if any one is in Christ, he is a new creation; the old has passed away, behold, the new has come" (2 Cor. 5:17). I wonder if we can ever fully realize how radical and how wonderful this is!

Both the letters of Paul and this word of exhortation to the Hebrews say to us that the system, the legalism, the old way of doing and redoing, trying and retrying, working and working harder—all these are done away with in Christ. Both the quest for righteousness under the law and the quest for forgiveness through sacrifice are seen to be ineffectual. Hebrews declares that both are antedated by God's promise, which is fulfilled in Christ, a priest forever after the order of Melchizedek. In him is our righteousness and our forgiveness.

### • Unchanging and Unending

The theme of Hebrews 7 is that those who have such a priest as Jesus have a savior whose saving power is without end. He is a priest who ministers "not according to a legal requirement concerning bodily descent but by the power of an indestructible life" (7:16). He has been raised from the dead and exercises his priesthood on our behalf continuously and forever.

The problem of every system or institution is that it never stays the same and eventually passes away. A vision creates an organization to fulfill a mission. But times change and leadership changes; subtle shifts in philosophy gradually erode the original purposes and goals. We have seen it happen to businesses, organizations, and universities.

So it was with the priesthood. It was always the intention to keep the lineage of the priests pure and their hearts sincere. Sometimes the goals were achieved, and many times they were not. The institutions of priesthood and sacrifice endured through the changing times and fortunes, but their meaning and effectiveness varied from age to age and from priest to priest. Sometimes priests would lead the people toward God and sometimes led them away. They were produced by the system and bound to the system, sinful men offering imperfect sacrifices for sinful people.

Then Jesus came, a priest of another order, not created by the system, not locked into the tradition, not bound by its functions. His loving concern, his atoning sacrifice for our sin, and his intercession are forever. What he is and what he has done are not passed on for others to complete. His once-for-all sacrifice for sin does not fall into other hands for fulfillment. He continues a priest forever. There is no delegation of authority, no break in continuity, no loss of effectiveness. Since his is the power of an indestructible life, no establishment can control his grace, no system can maneuver his forgiving love, no institution can manipulate the merits of his atoning death. Jesus' forever priesthood means that he is always the priest, he is always the sacrifice for sin, he is always the intercessor—yesterday, today, and forever.

## • Dimensions of Jesus' Priesthood

I would like to summarize three dimensions of Christ's priesthood that are mentioned in Hebrews 7.

The first is that through Jesus we can really come to God. "He is able for all time to save those who draw near to God through him" (7:25). Because he has been tempted as we are and can sympathize with our weaknesses, we can "draw near to the throne of grace, that we may receive mercy and find grace to help in time of need" (4:16). The old commandment, weak and useless, has been set aside and a better hope is introduced in Christ, "through which we draw near to God" (7:19). The sacrifices offered year after year can never "make perfect those who draw near" (10:1), but through the blood of Jesus and the living way he has opened as our great priest, we may "draw near with a true heart in full assurance of faith" (10:22).

From this perspective, it would seem that the whole purpose of the book of Hebrews is to bring us to God. We know that was the whole business of the priest. And Jesus our priest does precisely that very thing for us. He comes to us from God, comes all the way into our fallen humanity, and acts on our behalf to bring us to God. H. Orton Wiley used to say, "With one hand Jesus reaches into the heart of a loving father, with the other he reaches into the heart of a lost and broken humanity, and in himself he brings the two together."

The words of Fanny Crosby express the hunger of us all, "Draw me nearer, nearer, blessed Lord." Too many of us live with a sense of distance from God, feeling that we must somehow make ourselves worthy to find our way into his elusive presence. Can we know that Jesus is our priest, right where we are now? He is himself the way. Because Jesus is where we are, God is where we are, and the door is open.

The second dimension of Jesus' priesthood is that he really saves us from sin. "He holds his priesthood permanently, because he continues for ever. Consequently he is able for all time to save those who draw near to God through him" (7:24–25). Hebrews begins with the declaration that the Son, through whom God has spoken his final word, has "made purification for sins" (1:3); it closes by contrasting the burning of the bodies of animals sacrificed for sin with the suffering of Jesus "outside the gate in order to sanctify the people through his own blood" (13:12).

All through Hebrews, the reality to be faced and overcome is sin. Deceived by our sin, we can experience the hardening of heart that will destroy us. Sin that is deliberately and persistently committed separates us from the forgiveness of God. The message of Hebrews, however, is that God has come in Christ to deal with our sins in a way we never can. To forgive us, Jesus became like us "in every respect" (2:17). He "offered up himself" for our sins and in that self-offering accomplished what all the sacrifices through all the years could never do—take away sins (7:27; 10:4, 11–12).

We have a priest who is "holy, blameless, unstained, separated from sinners, exalted above the heavens. He has no need, like those high priests, to offer sacrifices daily, first for his own sins and then for those of the people; he did this once for all when he offered up himself" (7:26–27). That obedient self-offering and sacrifice becomes the vehicle for the offering of ourselves to God, making real in our lives forgiveness for sin.

The sacrifice of animals for our sins is as far removed from our culture as the priesthood of Melchizedek. What is not distant from our culture is our persistent effort to cover or ignore sins and our stubborn refusal to confess them in humility to God and receive the forgiveness offered through the death of Jesus our Savior. It was for our sins that he came; it was for our sins he died. Risen and reigning, our priest forever, he can truly forgive sin—old and deep sin, new and shallow sin. We may confess all sin to him. Isn't that what a priest is for? No more need sin separate us from God. Forgiven and clean, we may come with our high priest into his presence with confidence and joy.

The third dimension is that we have a priest who "is able for all time to save those who draw near to God through him, since he always lives to make intercession for them" (7:25). Jesus, who opens the way to God, who truly forgives sin, also makes intercession for us.

We are reminded of the "suffering servant" who, like a priest, "poured out his soul to death, and was numbered with the transgressors; yet he bore the sin of many, and made intercession for the transgressors" (Isa. 53:12). Paul tells us that the Spirit who knows both the heart of the Father and the hearts of men "intercedes for us with sighs too deep for words" (Rom. 8:26). He tells us that Jesus, our crucified and risen Lord, "intercedes for us" at the right hand of God (v. 34). Who, then, can condemn us?

## ● The Intercession of Jesus

These verses all give insight into our understanding of the intercession of Jesus. In Isaiah, the servant represents God, yet takes his place by the side of transgressors, to be counted with them, to die for them, and to intercede for them. Those who are guilty, who have no place to stand, who have no right to forgiveness, are the ones for whom the servant intercedes. In Romans 8:26 the Spirit of Christ intercedes for those who are weak and who do not know how to pray as they ought. In Romans 8:34 the crucified and exalted Christ intercedes for those who are vulnerable to the condemnation of the enemy. Our continuing priest intercedes for us in our transgressions, he prays for us when we are weak and do not know how to pray, and his prayers surround us when in our humanity we are susceptible to voices of accusation.

The intercession of the Son with the Father on our behalf is not to be understood as the effort to change the attitude or the posture of the Father toward us. Our priest does not seek by presenting himself or his petition to shift God's feelings from anger to kindness or from judgment to grace. Nor do we do so in our prayers for those we love. We do not pray against the will of God with the intention of changing it; rather, we pray earnestly for it and pour out our hearts to the Father, who loves those we love far more than we ever could and who hears us when we pray. Jesus, our priest who comes to take his place beside us, comes from the heart of the God against whom we have sinned. His very presence by our side and on our side testifies to the love and kindness of God, who does not wish "that any should perish, but that all should reach repentance" (2 Peter 3:9).

There are two dimensions of the intercession of Christ that are very significant to me. One aspect is the deep identification of Jesus our priest with us in our humanity. Having come and suffered and died, Jesus has not left us to our own devices or abandoned us to our own resources. He carries on the work of redemption by continuing identification with us at the very points of our guilt, weakness, and vulnerability. His intercession for us does not put him over against the Father. It does put him with us and for us as our friend and brother.

The other aspect is the continuing care of Jesus our priest. "He always lives to make intercession" for us (7:25). The more we care for others and the more earnestly we pray for them, the more aware we are of our inability to care and pray the way we want and should. We barely know how to pray a few things for ourselves, let alone bear the burdens of others. Do we realize that Jesus has undertaken to bear the burdens and cares and sins of the whole lot of us to the Father? He has made the final sacrifice for our sins and now continually loves, cares, and intercedes for us. He can save for all time because he is committed to us for all time.

That is the ground of our confident hope. When we are weak, he is still strong. When we do not know how to pray, he is still praying. When we are vulnerable to all kinds of condemning voices, he is still identified with us and still interceding for us. He is our priest forever.

## ● Discussion Questions

1. Reread Hebrews 7. Summarize the weaknesses of the Levitical priesthood and the sacrificial system. What illustrations can you give from your life of the way similar weaknesses have been present in religious systems or denominations?
2. Discuss the idea that for Christ to be the priest who really takes away sin means the end of the priesthood and sacrifice. Does this mean that these institutions had no meaning?
3. The way Christ does away with the sacrificial system in Hebrews has been compared with the way he does away with the law in Paul's

writings (Romans and Galatians). Do you find this comparison valid or helpful? Explain.

4. In modern terms, not using the religious vocabulary of Hebrews 7, what is the difference between a priesthood after the order of Aaron-Levi and a priesthood after the order of Melchizedek?

5. What does it mean to draw near, or come to God? How does Christ open the way for us?

6. Hebrews say a lot about sin and Christ's provision for it, but little about our repentance and faith. Why do you think this is the case? What guidance is there in Hebrews about receiving forgiveness of sins?

7. What does the intercession of Christ mean in your life?

8. Describe someone who has been a "Melchizedek" to you, that is, someone who has not really come from within the "system" or who has come from "outside," yet has been a priest to you, bringing you to the presence of God.

# CHAPTER · 9

# The New Covenant

Now the point in what we are saying is this: we have such a high priest, one who is seated at the right hand of the throne of the Majesty in heaven, a minister in the sanctuary and the true tent which is set up not by man but by the Lord. . . .

Christ has obtained a ministry which is as much more excellent than the old as the covenant he mediates is better, since it is enacted on better promises. . . .

"This is the covenant that I will make with the house of Israel after those days, says the Lord:
I will put my laws into their minds,
and write them on their hearts,
and I will be their God,
and they shall be my people.
And they shall not teach every one his fellow
or every one his brother, saying, 'Know the Lord,'
for all shall know me,
from the least of them to the greatest.
For I will be merciful toward their iniquities, and I will
remember their sins no more" [Jer. 31: 31–34].

In speaking of a new covenant he treats the first as obsolete. And what is becoming obsolete and growing old is ready to vanish away. . . .

But when Christ appeared as a high priest of the good things that have come, then through the greater and more perfect tent (not made with hands, that is, not of this creation) he entered once for all into the Holy Place, taking not the blood of goats and calves but his own blood, thus securing an eternal redemption. For if the sprinkling of defiled persons with the blood of goats and bulls and with the ashes of a heifer sanctifies

101

for the purification of the flesh, how much more shall the blood of Christ, who through the eternal Spirit offered himself without blemish to God, purify your conscience from dead works to serve the living God.

Therefore he is the mediator of a new covenant, so that those who are called may receive the promised eternal inheritance, since a death has occurred which redeems them from the transgressions under the first covenant. . . .

For Christ has entered, not into a sanctuary made with hands, a copy of the true one, but into heaven itself, now to appear in the presence of God on our behalf (Heb. 8:1–2, 6, 10—13; 9:11–15, 24).

● This passage of Scripture is not easily understood, but it has two basic points that need emphasizing: sacrifice for sin, and covenant bond with God.

Imagine yourself in the wilderness, in Old Testament times, standing on a hilltop, watching a ritual of sacrifice in the nearby tabernacle. You would observe a priest wash and robe himself, then you would see him sacrifice a young bull for the cleansing of his own sins and failures. You would see a worshiper bring an animal to the priest; he would place his hands on its head and then kill it. The priest would take the blood into the holy place and put it on the altar and around the base as an atonement for sin.

If you stayed in the wilderness long enough you would see this sort of ritual enacted day after day, week after week, month after month. Each year you would see the climax of these rituals in the great Day of Atonement when the priest crossed the veil into the Holy of Holies to make sacrifice for the sins of the nation.

What you could not see, on the Day of Atonement or any other day, is the heart of the priest or the penitence of the worshiper. Nor could you know the depths of their feelings of forgiveness or the quality of their inward relationship with God.

What would you have made of all that? Well, the writer to the Hebrews understood it all far better than we ever could, and we know what he thought. He knew that for all his preparation, a priest was never good enough or holy enough, nor did he ever live long enough, to be a truly adequate priest. The writer of Hebrews knew that underneath the repeated offerings was a hunger for a permanent and eternal sacrifice. The earthly symbols created a longing for the heavenly realities they stood for. Most of all, both priest and worshiper yearned for real and deep cleansing for sin and abiding fellowship with God.

The grand truth the writer knew was that Jesus is God's own answer to the hunger for an effectual priest, the longing for a real sacrifice for sin, and the yearning for deep forgiveness and a personal covenant bond with God.

Let me summarize the way the writer talks about the priestly ministry of Jesus in Hebrews 8:1–10:18. Jesus ministers in the heavenly sanctuary and mediates a new covenant (8:1–13). In the earthly sanctuary, a type of the heavenly one, the rituals reach a climax on the Day of Atonement, but they were never able to "perfect the conscience of the worshiper" (9:6–9). Christ, by his "once for all" entrance into the Holy Place and the offering of his own blood, secured the "eternal salvation" that purifies the conscience "from dead works to serve the living God" (9:11–14). Therefore he is the "mediator of a new covenant, so that those who are called may receive the promised eternal inheritance."

This is possible because through Jesus' death a real redemption or freedom from transgressions is available that was never experienced under the old covenant (9:15). Christ has entered "into heaven itself, now to appear in the presence of God on our behalf" (9:24). Having fulfilled the divine will in the offering of himself and being exalted at the right hand of the Father, Christ has the authority to mediate the new covenant, that is, the new relationship he has established with his people (10:1–18).

That is the summary. Now let's talk about its two great themes.

## • Once for All

The first theme is the once-for-all offering of Jesus as our sacrifice for sin. We should consider this against its historical background. According to the beliefs of ancient cultures outside

FAITH · FOR · THE · JOURNEY

Israel, mankind was created to serve the gods so that they could lead a carefree, divine life. Worship and sacrifices were designed to appease and to serve the gods so that the gods would in turn look kindly on the worshipers and keep them safe and prosperous. The society served the gods, and the gods preserved the culture. Sacrifices actually had a manipulative motive, getting the gods' attention, appeasing their anger, and soliciting their favor. The whole business was utilitarian.

There was nothing like this in Israel. Worship practices were not intended to exploit God. He needed no benefit from man. Nor were they performed to get his attention (as in the story of Elijah and the prophets of Baal in 1 Kings 18) or persuade him to act kindly. Israel's basic understanding of God was that he is good to his people; he does not need sacrifice in order to be moved to benevolence.

According to T. C. Vriezen, the sacrificial system in Israel existed to "maintain and purify the communion between man and God." The covenant relationship between God and Israel had already been established at Mount Sinai. Sacrifices and offerings were not *demanded* by him, but were *given* by him to enable his people to maintain communion with him through atonement. Sacrifice was the means by which the personal relationship was maintained, renewed, and restored between the holy God and his failing, sinning people. God himself took the initiative and provided the ways by which whatever distanced man from himself could be overcome.

We need to remember that the sacrifice in Israel was never intended to be mechanical or just going through the motions. What mattered was the personal response of the worshiper. The *obedient* performance of what God ordained made sacrifices effective, not their grandeur or frequency. No sacrifice worked "by itself." The worshiper's heart attitude was everything. The ritual was effective only when accompanied by genuine penitence and submission.

However, repentance and restitution were not enough. The *faithful* offering of the sacrifice was necessary. The worshiper could not save himself by either repentance or sacrifice. God's divine power reached down to save him in the moment when he offered himself with his sacrifice. In the case of burnt offerings and peace offerings, the worshiper identified himself with his offering by placing his hands on the head of the sacrificial animal (Lev. 1:3–17; 3:1–17; 6:8–13; 7:11–21, 28–36). The animal's offered life become the vehicle or means by which the worshiper offered himself to God.

There is no "theology of sacrifice" given to us in either the Old Testament or the New. Nowhere does God come to Israel to say, "This is what sacrifice is and this is why you will do it." Two or three summary statements can be made, however.

(1) Sacrifices for sin and guilt involved blood brought into contact with the altar. This is not because blood has some inherent power or magic, but because life is in the blood (Gen. 9:4–6; Lev. 17:11, 14). Blood shed is life given, life offered. The shedding of the blood of the sacrificial animal meant the offering of the life of the animal to God. In that process the worshiper offered his life to God.

(2) The ritual of shedding sacrificial blood kept the depth and seriousness of sin constantly in Israel's consciousness. Sin and death are inexorably bound together in this imagery, so sin could never be taken lightly. It could not be forgiven as a matter of course. It was a breach of covenant, a break in personal relationship with the holy God.

But while the idea of sacrifice is not very congenial to our Western ways of thinking, behind its stern and awful demands stands the loving heart of God who longs for the fellowship of his people. The holy God who cannot tolerate sin nevertheless provides the means by which sin can be removed and the sinner welcomed into fellowship.

(3) The writer to the Hebrews understood that all the preparations and observances of the sacrificial rituals in the tabernacle could not fully remove the sin of the penitent, nor could the blood of the sacrifices cleanse one's defiled conscience or break the grip of sin. The priest could not do for the sincere worshiper what was

needed most. The blood of animals could not wash away the inward stain, nor could sincere repentance compensate for the guilt of the past. One's restoration with God through sacrifice, though real, was always partial. The process was to be repeated again and again—an endless round of guilt and sacrifice. No wonder, then, that many finally just got tired and gave up, or settled for rote observance of external rituals.

We can understand the urgency of the writer of Hebrews to declare something more than endless, inadequate ritual. That is the way my neighbor looks at churchgoing, as external, perfunctory, repeated ritual. And he says no thanks. But there is more, much more. God has come to us in his Son, who offered himself as our final and sufficient sacrifice for sin. All that was symbolized and anticipated in the repeated offerings of the past has now come to fulfillment in Christ. The death of Christ, the shedding of his blood on the cross, is his willing, obedient offering of his life to God on our behalf.

Our identification with Christ in his death is not merely a symbolic act like placing hands on an animal, but the real identification of ourselves with him in personal relationship. Christ's death as a sacrifice is not a ritualistic act. At the heart of it is the Son's obedient and submissive response to his Father, in an act that is the ultimate expression of personal relationship. Our identification with him in his death is the obedient and submissive offering of ourselves to him in personal relationship.

In the old system God provided the means by which the worshiper could approach him. In Christ, God provides *himself* as the means of forgiveness and fellowship. God's holy revulsion against sin and God's holy love for the sinner meet at the cross. There the offended God offers himself in sacrificial love and opens the way for us to come to him. "For if the sprinkling of defiled persons with the blood of goats and bulls and with the ashes of a heifer sanctifies for the purification of the flesh, how much more shall the blood of Christ, who through the eternal Spirit offered himself without blemish to God, purify your conscience from dead works to serve the living God" (Heb. 9:13–14; also 10:19–23).

## • The New Covenant

The second major theme of this Hebrews passage is that the sacrificial system was designed to maintain, renew, and restore the covenant relationship.

Let's talk about that wonderful word "covenant." A covenant is a solemn agreement between persons or groups who desire a personal relationship. It is based on promises made and kept, and it is kept alive by loyalty. It is not like a contract, which is based on expected benefits, arrived at by negotiated stipulations, and has a termination date. A business deal is by contract; a good marriage is by covenant. The latter is like our relationship with God.

The Hebrews understood that. From ancient times they had understood themselves to be in a special relationship with God because he had made a covenant with them. That covenant had some distinctive features. It was not a mutually-agreed-upon arrangement between equals; God was the originator. He took the initiative and called Abraham, promising to make him a nation, give him land and name, and through him bless the whole world. After the great deliverance in the Exodus, God reaffirmed the covenant relationship at Mount Sinai, saying to the people, "I will be your God. You shall be my people." It was a personal relationship grounded in love and a desire for fellowship.

When once entered by appropriate ritual and acceptance of conditions, however, it became a mutually binding agreement. Israel's self-understanding was based on this covenant bond. The people knew themselves to be the people of God. He was their God—he had bound himself to be God to them. They were his people and had bound themselves to be a people to him, responding to him through worship and the kind of lifestyle expressed in the Ten Commandments.

We can readily see that if the relationship between them had been a contract, it would have ended almost before it began, for the Hebrews were a recalcitrant and sinning people. But covenant is based on personal relationship and sustained by love and loyalty—like a marriage. God was forgiving and long-suffering, giving them the sacrificial system as the means of expressing both their thankful praise and their repentant confession of sin.

The tragic reality is that in spite of the faithfulness of God through the centuries, their persistent disobedience and rebellion strained and finally broke the covenant bond. Israel was a broken people with a broken covenant.

Yet the Hebrew writer understood and was insistent to say that when all was lost, God in awesome faithfulness promised a new covenant, actualized through the sacrificial death and the priestly mediation of Jesus Christ, his own Son. This new covenant is vastly superior to the old. The writer demonstrates this through a remarkable series of contrasts and comparisons between the two.

These distinctions place an earthly tabernacle over against a heavenly one (9:1–5). One covenant is external, the other internal (9:10, 13). The external covenant is temporary, operating in the interim; the heavenly one is lasting and eternal (9:9–10). The blood of thoughtless, unwilling animals is contrasted with the purposeful and willing sacrifice of the Son of God (9:12–14). The sacrifices of the old covenant are repetitive and incomplete; Christ's death is a final, once-for-all offering (9:25–26). The priests stood in the sanctuary to minister; Christ sits in royal authority at God's right hand, for his sacrifice has been accomplished (8:1; 10:11–12).

Under the old covenant, the Book of the Law, the sanctuary, the vessels, and the people were all consecrated by the sprinkling of blood. Under the new covenant, the stamp of the blood of Christ is upon all our relationships, our selves, our worship and conduct, our fellowship with others; the stamp of the cross is upon them all. In Rudolf Bultmann's beautiful phrase, the whole of life is "marked with the seal of consecration" (see 9:19–28).

## ● Four Promises in the New Covenant

There are four significant elements of the promised new covenant quoted in Hebrews.

(1) The first is that the initiative of God creates a covenant community undergirded by the grand covenant formula "I will be their God and they shall be my people." Six times in 8:8–12, God's promise is declared: "I will establish a new covenant . . . I will make . . . I will put my laws into their minds . . . I will be their God . . . I will be merciful . . . I will remember their sins no more."

These great promises were given right at the point of old Israel's total failure and inability. They were recalled to the first readers of Hebrews in the time of their discouragement and listlessness. The new covenant is the ground of identity and security because it does not rest on human initiative and ability but upon God's gracious promise demonstrated in Christ. He has made his promise, he has fulfilled his promise, he will keep his promise. That good news of Hebrews is good for us all.

(2) The second is the promise of inward power that overcomes our inability to obey the will of God. "I will put my laws into their minds, and write them on their hearts" (8:10). The new relationship is not external and mechanical. God is our God, we are his people. We are not merely offered a certain legal status with God; we are granted an inward relationship that is moral and spiritual, intimate and mutual.

If the new covenant is to be new, something has got to be different. God did not say that the old covenant was not good; his complaint was that his people "did not continue" in it (8:9). What will make us any different than they? The internalizing of the will of God. It is a change within us that we ourselves cannot create, but is brought about by the quality and intimacy of personal relationship with God that we have in Jesus.

Rule keeping and external conformity may produce acceptable behavior, but they never fulfill the divine intention for intimate, loving fellowship. They never satisfy our hunger for free and joyful relationship. The achievements are never quite adequate, and the effort eventually becomes too burdensome to continue. The gracious promise of God is that his Spirit will work from within, conforming our wills to his will and enabling us to live in freedom, from the inside and not by external conformities.

(3) The third element in the new covenant is the promise of universal knowledge of God. Both Jews and Gentiles of all kinds may share intimate, personal relationship with him. There is no privileged class. From the least to the greatest, from "babes" (Matt. 11:25) to the mature, relationship with God may be real and authentic. Too many of us feel that people in the ministry or special "religious" vocations have an access to God that is not available to ordinary folk. But the knowledge of the "least" is as valid as the knowledge of the "greatest."

The sacrifice of Christ in the heavenly tabernacle universalizes his priestly ministry. It takes it out of a special place to a special people and opens it up to the whole world. Knowing God is not the privilege of the few, nor is it in the control of the few. Knowing him is neither theoretical nor mediated through other people, but instead is direct, personal, and experiential. And it is for all.

(4) The fourth element is one that has been emphasized again and again in Hebrews: the forgiveness of sins (1:3; 2:17; 5:1; 8:12; 9:11–14, 26, 28; 10:2, 4–7, 11–15, 17). No book in the New Testament speaks more seriously about sin and its awful power to deceive and destroy. None speaks more forcefully about the reality of God's provision for the forgiveness of sins and the cleansing of the heart and conscience.

The Hebrews were not told they were bad people because they were sinners. Remember, they were believers who had left their past at great cost to follow Jesus, but were growing discouraged and tired; they were losing heart and nerve and were in danger of quitting. At this point they did not need to hear that they were sinners as much as they needed to hear and hear and hear that God does indeed forgive sin, that his forgiveness is real and all-pervasive. They needed to believe in their high priest and to know in their own experience that he has made the final sacrifice for all their sin. They needed assurance that he intercedes in their behalf with infinite love and patience.

There are times when we need to be told how deep and real and serious sin is. Most of us, most of the time, already know that. What we find hard to believe is that our sin in its depth and seriousness can really be forgiven and cleansed. We desperately need to know that our destructive guilt and sin—of yesterday, of ten years ago or fifty years ago—can be fully forgiven and our hearts be truly cleansed and healed. This is the assurance of the new covenant. We may live in humility and confidence before others and before God "With hearts made pure and garments white, / And Christ enthroned within" (Phoebe Palmer Knapp).

All this has been promised by God, supported by his oath, and guaranteed in the new covenant through the atoning work of Christ. I am not alone in observing that these gracious and joyful realities are not readily discernible in the lives of many who make up the church of Christ today. In concluding this chapter I want to emphasize one aspect of our subject that I believe explains why much "old covenant" existence remains within the "new covenant" reality. This aspect is the continuing priestly ministry of Christ.

## ● Conclusion

There is more to be said than that a new covenant has been established. Its glory is that it is continually *mediated,* that is, it is made constantly effectual through the identification with us and the intercession for us of the one who is our sacrifice for sin.

As we walk, forgiven and restored, into the future, he walks with us ministering the covenant. He is present with us on the journey, mediating and actualizing the grace and mercy we have received, being to us what a priest is—our sacrifice, brother, and intercessor. We are absolutely dependent upon his life and his work. Our victory is rooted in his continuing mediation of his once for all sacrifice for our sins. Apart from that ministry we are back in the old rut, needing repeated sacrifices for repeated failures and sins.

"Therefore, brethren [and sisters], since we have confidence to enter the sanctuary by the blood of Jesus, by the new and living way which he opened for us . . . through his flesh, and since we have a great priest over the house of God, let us draw near with a true heart in full assurance of faith, with our hearts sprinkled clean from an evil conscience and our bodies washed with pure water. Let us hold fast the confession of our hope without wavering, for he who promised is faithful (10:19–23).

## ● Discussion Questions

1. In pagan religions, people offer sacrifices to the gods to appease them and to entice them to bring some desired result in personal life and society. According to this definition, in what ways do some Christians still have "pagan" ideas of the sacrifice of Christ?

2. Of what importance is it for us to understand that, although people performed the specific acts and rituals, God himself gave them the sacrificial system as a means of enhancing their relationship with him?

3. I have suggested that the sacrificial animal was not offered strictly as a substitute for the worshiper. That is, it was not offered "instead" of the worshiper, but as a means for the worshiper to offer *himself*. Discuss this idea.

4. What are some of the ways Christ fulfills the symbols and meanings of Old Testament sacrifice? What things are new or different in his self-offering for sin?

5. Discuss the idea that God himself provides the way for rebellious mankind to come to him—and that way is himself. Does Christ's death change the attitude of God toward the sinner?

6. Why is it important to see the differences between contract and covenant for our understanding of our relationship with God? Why would contract arrangements in marriage not work? What are some contract-type deals we might be tempted to make with God?

7. Is "covenant" a helpful way to consider one's relationship to his church? How might the family be changed if we thought of it in terms of covenant?

8. I have mentioned four significant elements in the new covenant. Which of them means the most in terms of your relationship with God?

# CHAPTER · 10

# Faith for the Journey

But recall the former days when, after you were enlightened, you endured a hard struggle with sufferings, sometimes being publicly exposed to abuse and affliction, and sometimes being partners with those so treated. For you had compassion on the prisoners, and you joyfully accepted the plundering of your property, since you knew that you yourselves had a better possession and an abiding one. Therefore do not throw away your confidence, which has a great reward. For you have need of endurance, so that you may do the will of God and receive what is promised. . . .

But we are not of those who shrink back and are destroyed, but of those who have faith and keep their souls.

Now faith is the assurance of things hoped for, the conviction of things not seen. For by it the men of old received divine approval. . . . And without faith it is impossible to please him. For whoever would draw near to God must believe that he exists and that he rewards those who seek him. . . .

These all died in faith, not having received what was promised, but having seen it and greeted it from afar, and having acknowledged that they were strangers and exiles on the earth. For people who speak thus make it clear that they are seeking a homeland. If they had been thinking of that land from which they had gone out, they would have had opportunity to return. But as it is, they desire a better country, that is, a heavenly one. Therefore God is not ashamed to be called their God, for he has prepared for them a city. . . .

And all these, though well attested by their faith, did not receive what was promised, since God had foreseen something better for us, that apart from us they should not be made perfect.

Therefore, since we are surrounded by so great a cloud of witnesses, let us also lay aside every weight, and sin which clings so closely, and let us run with perseverance the race that is set before us, looking to Jesus the pioneer and perfecter of our faith (Heb. 10:32–36, 39; 11:1–2, 6, 13–16, 39–40; 12:1–2).

● In hard times, it is good to remember other times. Can you remember the experience of being a newborn child of God, or the experience of things turning out better than you thought, or discovering that there was, after all, good stuff in you? Such memories have life-changing power in the present.

The Hebrews needed to remember. They had heard a dark warning (10:26–31). What if they should fail? "No," says the writer, "recall the former days!" Those had been hard days, but good ones. The Hebrews had endured suffering, public shame, and exploitation. They not only took it grandly, but were at the same time being compassionate partners of others. There is probably no greater example of the mind and spirit of Christ found in the New Testament. They had experienced real enlightenment, real suffering and real victory.

The exhortation is, "Don't throw away your confidence now!" James Moffatt's commentary voices the challenge, "The storm burst on them early, they weathered it nobly: why give up the voyage when it is nearly done?" Fulfillment of the promise is sure and will come soon. The righteous live by faith—that is, they hold fast to the relationship they have been given and keep faith in the sure promises of God. A faith that hangs on and keeps confidence will sustain life and receive the sure promise.

Hebrews 11, the great faith chapter with its famous roll call of heroes, needs to be read in this context.

● Faith Is a Promise

The congregation to whom the book of Hebrews was written were experiencing a crisis of faith and needed to remember—to call into the present—the kind of enlightenment, endurance, and hope with which they began their Christian pilgrimage. They also needed to recall the former, former days of their ancestors in faith. They needed to see themselves as present participants in the great fellowship of those pioneers who, in their own dispensation, had seen the promises, became persuaded of them, and embraced them.

Those pioneers had placed their hopes in God, made their commitment, and confessed their alien posture to the values of this world. They never actually "cashed in" on the promises, yet they were sustained in joy and in real relationship with God. They endured in faith and assurance, confident that the promises were real and that their vision of the future was valid.

"Now faith is the assurance of things hoped for, the conviction of things not seen" (11:1). This famous definition of faith is given in the context of the situation of the Hebrews and consistent with the writer's exhortations in the preceding verses. It is a description of the faith of those who "do not shrink back" but endure and "keep their souls" (10:39).

Faith is the certainty that the hopes grounded in the promises of God will come true. It is also the conviction, in William Barclay's words, "that the unseen and invisible realities not only exist, but are the most important things of all." Or to use William Manson's phrasing, faith recognizes what the writer to the Hebrews calls "invisible" things "as the supreme realities" and makes them "determinative" for life. This kind of faith is a living and effective power in the life of the Christian pilgrim. The certainty of hope and the conviction of God's unseen realities enable us to act and move on into the future, whatever it holds, and endure.

Let's talk about the faith chapter by beginning at the end. "Therefore, since we are surrounded by so great a cloud of witnesses . . ." (12:1). The first image that comes to mind is that of a stadium filled with spectators witnessing the race being run by the Christians. I can visualize the saints who have gone before looking down over the battlements of heaven. They have finished their course and are watching and waiting for us to finish ours and join them. I think there is truth in this kind of imagery.

Note first that the word translated "witnesses" is the word for "martyrs." In the verb form the word means "to bear witness." Martyrs were people who declared their faith and sometimes died for it. A witness is not a spectator, but one who has something to say and gives testimony. That great cloud of witnesses who surround the Christian pilgrims, who believed God, trusted the promises, endured the journey, and finally triumphed, have something to say; their lives are shouting out to us the meaning and significance of faith.

● Faith Is a Verb

I hear from these witnesses two fundamental truths. The first is, faith is not something you have, it is something you do. All through this chapter of Hebrews, faith is defined by behavior, by the way choices are made and values are expressed. The subject is faith, but the men and women mentioned are characterized by their actions in the real world.

Look at the verbs. By faith Abel "*offered* to God" an acceptable sacrifice (v. 4). Enoch (v. 5) "*walked* with God" (Gen. 5:22, 24). By faith Noah "*took heed* and *constructed* an ark . . . and became an heir of the righteousness which comes by faith" (v. 7). By faith Abraham "*obeyed* when he was called to go out . . . and he *went out* . . . he *sojourned* in the land of promise, . . . *living* in tents . . . for he *looked forward* to a city which has foundations" (vv. 8–10).

Abraham's descendants died without receiving what was promised, but they *saw* and "*greeted* it from afar, and "*acknowledged* that they were strangers and exiles on the earth" (v. 13). "By faith Abraham, when he was tested, *offered* up Isaac, and he who had received the promises *was ready to offer* up his only son . . . He *considered* that God was able to raise men, even from the dead" (vv. 17–19).

"By faith Moses, when he was born, *was hid* for three months by his parents, . . . they *were not afraid* of the king's edict" (v. 23). "By faith Moses, when he was grown up, *refused . . . choosing . . .* he *considered . . . he looked* to the reward" (vv. 24–26). "By faith he *left* Egypt, *not being afraid . . .* he *endured* as *seeing* him who is invisible *. . .* he *kept* the Passover and *sprinkled* the blood . . . by faith the people *crossed* the Red Sea" (vv. 27–29). The walls of Jericho "*fell down,* " and Rahab did not perish because by faith she "*had given* friendly *welcome* to the spies" (vv. 30–31).

The next paragraph of Hebrews 11 is filled with vivid and lively words of action, describing the faith of those "for whom time would fail" to tell. They "*conquered . . . enforced* justice, *received* promises, *stopped* the mouths of lions, *quenched* raging fire, *escaped* the edge of the sword, *won* strength . . . *became mighty . . . put* foreign armies *to flight,*" and women "*received* their dead by resurrection" (vv. 32–35).

The writer then speaks of faith heroes of another kind, perhaps more congenial to the Hebrews' own feelings about themselves. He describes not so much the action of their faith as the reflex action of others because of their faith. "Some *were tortured, refusing* to accept release . . . others *suffered* mocking and scourging, and even chains of imprisonment. They *were stoned . . . sawn in two . . . killed . . . went about* in skins . . . *destitute, afflicted, ill-treated . . . wandering* over deserts and mountains, and in dens and caves of the earth" (vv. 36–38)—and the world could not hold a candle to them!

A review of this remarkable list of verbs reemphasizes that faith is not something we have, it is something we do. Faith is how we offer, how we walk, how we listen, and how we build. It is hearing when we are called and obeying when it is time to go. It is living in the knowledge that this world is not our home.

## • Faith Is a Journey to Who Knows Where

Faith is sometimes an obedient and somber journey to the mountain of surrender. It is the certainty of vision that will bless one's children and send them down the road toward an unknown destination with confidence only in God. Sometimes it means defiance of a royal order, sometimes refusal, sometimes a choice between rewards. And it means not being afraid. A time or two in life it might mean an obedient and symbolic act done without any surety of the outcome. The first Passover was like that.

Walls have fallen down by faith; so have kingdoms as justice has prevailed. God's faithful people have accomplished marvelous things by faith; they have experienced great deliverance and done the impossible. God's people have also been true and loyal and full of faith when no walls have fallen down. They have sometimes experienced great suffering and sorrow.

In any case, the faith of God's people is their way of looking, of responding, of living and deciding and acting. It is their process of evaluating or choosing alternatives and priorities in line with their vision of God and his purposes. Faith, then, needs a verbal form— something like "faithing."

A strange man is pounding in the pegs, framing the monstrous boat in his backyard. "What are you doing, Noah?" *"I'm faithing!"*

"Old man, where are you going? Everyone else seems to be coming." *"I'm not really sure."* "Why are you leaving the good life behind?" *"Well, there was this voice—and I've got a promise."* "What are you doing, Abraham?" *"I'm faithing!"*

"Where are you headed, Moses?" *"I'm off to see the Pharaoh."* "The terrible Pharaoh of Egypt?" *"Yes."* "Why?" *"Well, there was this bush—and I've got a command."* "What are you doing?" *"I'm faithing!"*

"All of you pilgrims out there, wandering around in deserts and hiding in the caves, you could ease up a little in your commitment to your invisible God and save yourselves a lot of this trouble and suffering." *"Yes, we know."* "How are you able to keep your values straight in the middle of all this stress and hardship? You haven't even seen what it is you are hoping for." *"We're faithing!"*

Robert Jewett points out that the response of faith to the call of God is made in the context of the secular world. The behavior of those who heard and obeyed, from an ordinary point of view, was not "religious" (look again at the list of verbs). They were not in church surrounded by supporting friends. They were in an otherwise-minded society and had to face the alienation and suffering of going against popular opinion. They walked and built and obeyed, made their choices, and took their licks in a secular culture. They didn't just "have" their faith, they "did" it.

## ● Faith Is Endurance

The cloud of witnesses is shouting out another fundamental meaning of faith—endurance in hope. The paragraph beginning at 11:32 summarizes some marvelous victories of faith. The heroes triumphed in the face of hostile kings, injustice, lions, fire, sword, and the foreign legion—even death!

A casual reading of verse 35 can miss the profound shift in direction and emphasis. "Women received their dead by resurrection. *Some were tortured,* refusing to accept release, that they might rise again to a better life." The paragraph describes the sufferings and severe trials of God's faithful pilgrims. They were the ragtags and nobodies of society, ill-treated wanderers in a world unworthy of them. All these—the ones who triumphed and the ones who suffered—were "well attested by their faith" (11:39).

It would be common in our day to characterize these sufferers as people whose ordeal demonstrates the need for more faith. But the author of Hebrews has a different view. In 10:32–35 he recalls the early days of the Hebrews' "enlightenment" and how it brought struggle and suffering. They needed to remember that the love you give doesn't always come back and your outstretched hand to feed can get bitten. We need to know that truth as well.

We think that if we show the love of Jesus, everyone will love us; if we have faith, we will be healthy, have money to satisfy all our desires, and have happiness in our security. We think our troubles will be over if we give our lives to Jesus—but the truth is, they may have just begun. We want to hear only of victories, not sufferings; but Hebrews tells us that both are part of the pilgrim life of the Christian. When faith is defined in terms of visible victories and material gain, it reflects not the word of the Bible but the word of our selfish desires. How can true faith emerge in such a context?

Faith is endurance. It is hope that will not let go in the midst of trial. In this epistle we learn that faith and hope almost inevitably produce suffering, and faith means the endurance of suffering in the confidence of our hope.

I see it this way: Faith brings us into real and personal relationship with God; it keeps us in continuing dialogue with him. God is the center of our lives and the final focus of our attention. Our relationship with him calls us into the orbit of his concerns and purposes. In the language of Hebrews, we are called to a pilgrimage, called to participate in the journey of God's people toward the "promised land," that is, toward the fulfillment of his goals for his redeemed world. Ultimately the goal is heaven.

The basic perspective, then, is toward the future. The whole of Hebrews has this future orientation. The Son is "heir of all things" (1:2). The Son's lordship will last until all enemies have been put under his feet (1:13). The Son is lord over the "world to come" (2:5). We have "tasted the powers of the age to come" (6:5) and are to "hope until the end" (6:11). We are encouraged to "seize the hope set before us" (6:18). Christ "will appear a second time . . . to save those who are eagerly waiting for him" (9:28). We need to encourage one another, "and all the more as you see the Day drawing near" (10:25).

The heroes of faith in chapter 11 are called out of and away from their past into the future of God's provision. They walk into that future not by sight but by the vision of faith that sees what is invisible and appropriates it into the present life as the governing force. People involved wholeheartedly in this kind of pilgrimage do not walk the ways of their surrounding culture. Their values and their goals, their life and commitment, put them at odds with a world without hope trying to live without faith.

Can we see that faith, far from delivering us from trouble, is what often brings us into trouble? Our faith is expressed in our enduring that trouble as we continue our journey of hope. The writer to the Hebrews held before them, in their discouragement, the example of their suffering, enduring, hoping forefathers. Many, like Abraham and Moses and the prophets, saw the vision, heard the voice, answered the call, and began the journey. They left all else behind and threw their lives away for their faith. They suffered, struggled, were crushed down, and got steam-rollered in the end—but they never gave up. They lived for the promise— and they died before they ever saw its fulfillment. They lived as pilgrims, sustained by a promise and upheld by a vision. They died without ever seeing their dreams or their hopes come true—but they never quit, never let go. And God said, "I am not ashamed to be called their God!"

## ● Conclusion

These witnesses have something to say to us, all right. They shout it out in confidence and joy because the one for whom they looked has come; the promise has been fulfilled. The vision for which they lived and died did not tarry forever. Jesus Christ, the incarnate Word, our high priest and sacrifice for sin, fulfilled the promises and inaugurated the kingdom. In these days we join with those witnesses—with those Hebrews and with all the saints of the intervening ages—in the journey of faith, looking toward the consummation. We, too, walk by faith expressed in how we act and build and offer and choose and refuse and esteem—and how we endure and persevere and hope and hang on.

There are some who say, "I have faith. What they mean is, "I am believing God to give me a job and heal my ills and grant me the desires of my heart for love and security and money and happiness." Some may say, "I don't think I have much faith." Yet they are making choices, evaluations, and decisions as they live and work in the world. They are seeking to set the right priorities, find the real values, and follow the Christ style of life. To them God draws near to say, "I am not ashamed to be called your God!"

## • Discussion Questions

Read all of Hebrews 11 before taking up the questions that follow.

1. It is good for us to remember our early Christian days, whether recent or distant. What are your memories? How do your early experiences relate to those of the Hebrews? Why is it that when early Christian emotions fade, often confidence and hope also fade?

2. From your reading of Hebrews 11:1, how would you define faith? Does faith make invisible things real? How would our general views of faith change if we made 11:32 the beginning of chapter 11?

3. What mental images do you get as you read Hebrews 12:1–2? Put in your own words what you think the author was trying to communicate by citing these heroes.

4. I have emphasized faith not as something we have, but as something we do. Discuss this idea. How would you relate faith as illustrated in Hebrews to the Christian teaching that we are "saved by faith" (as in Eph. 2:8)?

5. From your own experience and in your own words, how would you define or illustrate "faithing?"

6. In Hebrews, those who triumphed and those who suffered are placed on equal ground as heroes of faith. What would that say to those first readers? What about us? How can we free ourselves from the idea that faith can bring us the "good life"?

7. What does it mean that faith is endurance? In what sense does just plain not quitting express faith?

8. Many people tend to think they don't have faith because good things are not happening to them or because bad things are. What would you say to these people in the light of the teaching of Hebrews 11?

# CHAPTER · 11

# Looking to Jesus

And all these, though well attested by their faith, did not receive what was promised, since God had foreseen something better for us, that apart from us they should not be made perfect.

Therefore, since we are surrounded by so great a cloud of witnesses, let us also lay aside every weight, and sin which clings so closely, and let us run with perseverance the race that is set before us, looking to Jesus the pioneer and perfecter of our faith, who for the joy that was set before him endured the cross, despising the shame, and is seated at the right hand of the throne of God (Heb. 11:39–12:2).

● In the faith chapter the writer opens the eyes of the Hebrews to the great cloud of witnesses that surrounds them. That cloud is a crowd of God's faithful pilgrims who in the past journeyed into the unknown with confidence and courage. They endured the hardships without giving up their expectation that the promises to which they committed their lives would be fulfilled. All through their long journey, generation after generation, the promises were seen and embraced, lived out, and passed on. None of them ever lived to see their fulfillment, yet they never gave up faith and hope. That is why they served as such great examples for the discouraged members of the Hebrew congregation.

But there is more to it than that. The writer, with great historical perspective, saw that their pilgrimage, though faltering and threatened, was yet part of the framework of God's saving purposes throughout history. The ancient heroes of faith were participants in those purposes, but they were not "made perfect" apart from the community of believing Hebrews. The witnesses were not just "back there" in the past, good examples of great faith. They and the Hebrews belonged to the same company of pilgrims. The God who worked in the past was working in their present, continuing to accomplish his will.

The old saints had their journey, the Hebrews were in the process of theirs, and now, these many centuries later, we are in the process of ours. But the prime truth is that God has a journey, too! And it is his journey in which we participate.

## • A Race to Run

Each of us runs the race and makes the pilgrimage in the context of the great purposes of God, who calls us into covenant partnership and conversation with him. The old heroes were not made perfect without the Hebrew community; and the latter in turn are not made perfect without us; and we in turn, not apart from the host of Christian pilgrims who surround us. We make our personal journey as partners in the saving journey of God through the world's history on the way to the final redemption.

The writer of Hebrews also has a great personal perspective. He understands that God fulfills his saving purposes in the dynamic of personal relationships. God works in freedom to save us, and he works with us in the context of our freedom to accomplish his will. He works in the context of the choices, good and bad, of his people in the real world. That means it always takes longer than we think it is going to, and that is why the exhortations and warnings are to be taken as seriously as the promises.

The sovereign will of God does not pick and choose and use us as pawns on the gameboard of history. He calls us into personal relationship and conversation with him and works with us through the changing scenes of history and the changing scenes of our own life's story. We are weak and prone to discouragement—we need the promises. We are self-serving and prone to drift—we need the exhortations and the warnings. The marvel of God's grace is that he gives us both as he works and waits and loves, giving us our freedom while working out his will.

Surrounded as we are by the great host of witnesses, we are to "lay aside every weight, and sin which clings so closely," and "run with perseverance the race that is set before us" (12:1). It seems to me that the image of the Christian life as a race is both good and bad. If it conjures up the false idea that the Christian life means constant sweating and straining to keep ahead of the competition, then it is not helpful. It is bad if it suggests that we must keep trying harder to please God lest we fail.

This is good imagery, however, because it expresses the dynamic, moving, changing character of our pilgrimage. The words are trite, but the truth is vital: If we are not going forward, we are drifting. There is a journey to be made, there are struggles to endure, battles to be fought, joys to be experienced, praise to be given. And there is discipline to be accepted. God has a plan, we are going somewhere, and there is a goal to be achieved.

## ● Running Is the Goal

Our race is in fact "set before us" (12:1). The process of the race is as much a providential appointment as the achievement of the goal. The race is given to us. I remember, in my early years as a college chaplain, feeling that we had to get our discipline problems solved, our institutional goals clear, and all our faculty and students fully committed to them so that we could be a "Christian college." If we could just get rid of the conflicting and contradictory elements in our community, we could get on with the business of being the kind of college God wanted us to be. Both experience and this Letter to the Hebrews have taught me to think differently. Being a Christian college community means being engaged in the process of learning and solving problems and facing issues from the perspective of our understanding of Christ and the gospel. For that matter, being a Christian family means being involved in the very process of working out the hassles and heartaches of ordinary life, trying to find and do the will of God.

To be a Christian is surely not to have solved all the problems; it is commitment to Christ and faithfulness to him through all the trials and temptations and decisions by which Christian life is developed. In the language of Hebrews, the race is the course ordained for us in the achievement of the goal. The Christian life means hanging on in the process of making it through the course.

If we deny the process or chafe because problems have to be dealt with or issues faced, we can miss the means by which God would work with us to make us the mature Christians we want to become. If we reject the validity of God's presence in the flow of ordinary life, we can fall easily into the "if only" habit. If only my house were different; if only my family were different; if only I had more time or better work or more money or better health. Truth is, we are where we are, we are what we are. There is a race before us to be run, a course to traverse, in reaching the goal.

The message of Hebrews is that our Savior is our brother, our priest, and our companion on the way. We do not run alone; there is a great crowd of witnesses around us as we go step by step, day by day, facing the problems and meeting the issues. The course is to be affirmed and embraced as God's providential appointment. It is the designated way by which we reach our final destination.

The exhortation to run our race with perseverance points us to the long view. The title of Eugene Peterson's splendid book expresses it precisely: *A Long Obedience in the Same Direction*. Most of us in our consumer-oriented society are so influenced by advertisers that we believe we can have what we really want without either waiting or working for it. Perseverance belongs to the select few whose specific goals demand it. The long-distance runner, the elitist scholar, the master musician, the ivory carver, the injured athlete determined to walk again—these persons need perseverance. They cannot depend on or be governed by their emotions; day in and day out they must keep at it. The rest of us operate mostly by the pendulum swings of our whims, moods, and desires. Perseverance, or "stick-to-it-iveness," has little appeal.

The word takes us immediately out of the realm of emotions and puts us into the realm of will. Actually the emotional dynamics of the Christian life are not much different than those of ordinary life. There are certain emotions attached to beginnings—the joy of a birth, the excitement of a wedding, the start of a job, a new beginning in a new location. There is a certain kind of feeling that comes to those who stand at the blocks or at the pool's edge just before the race. There is a different set of emotions that goes with the mid-time. And the feelings at the end are not like any other.

Most of us are somewhere in the mid-time of our Christian race, and Hebrews would say to us that the right word is not necessarily "ecstasy" or "excitement" or "thrill." The right word is "persevere." That means keeping on and hanging on and carrying on with "long obedience in the same direction."

## • Traveling Light

"Therefore, since we are surrounded by so great a cloud of witnesses, let us also lay aside every weight, and sin which clings so closely, and let us run with perseverance the race that is set before us" (v. 1). The word "weight" is a simple word that means "bulk" or "mass." If you are engaged in the long run, you don't add weight, you take it off. When you come to the blocks to run the relay race, you don't put your robe on, you take it off, because it is a weight that hinders the running. When you come to the edge of the pool, you don't wrap the towels around you, you take them off; they are weights that encumber your swimming. Whatever it is that hinders us in our Christian race is a weight to be put off.

I can see the Christian pilgrim running up the shining way, clutching his robe and sash tightly around him. His spindly legs are pumping as he pounds the turf. He is on his way, looking like a wiseman-escapee from the Sunday school Christmas program. Soon his sash comes loose, and his robe begins to flap in the breeze. It trips him and he falls. He gets up, gathers up, puts on a Band-Aid, and starts running again. Soon the wind loosens the folds of his robe. Down again he goes. And we are too much like him! We have started the journey, but we are carrying too much, bearing too much, doing too much, failing too much. We stumble and fall, get up, wrap up, pick up, and struggle on.

It is not always easy to know what the weights are. In Romans 13:12 Paul says, "Let us then cast off the works of darkness." In Ephesians 4:22, 25, we are told to put off our "old nature" and "put away falsehood." In Colossians 3:8 we are exhorted to "put them all away, anger, wrath, malice, slander, and foul talk from your mouth." First Peter 2:1 tells us the same thing. James 1:21 exhorts us to "put away all filthiness and rank growth of wickedness." These verses may give us a clue about what the New Testament church believed Christians need to "lay aside."

We wish we knew what weights the pioneers of faith in the Old Testament had to lay aside in order to follow the promise. We do know some of the deep concerns of the pastor-author of Hebrews for his people. They were hindered by drift (2:1), by neglect (2:3), by unbelief and hardness of heart (3:12, 19; 4:11), by dullness of hearing (5:11), sluggishness (6:12), loss of confidence and shrinking back (10:35, 39). I wish these old verses were not such an accurate description of today's ordinary church member.

If a weight is anything that hinders us on our journey, I believe that the best way to find out what it is, is to start running. That is, begin to listen seriously and attentively to the word of God our covenant partner, to diligently participate in the dialogue into which he calls us with serious intent to obey. Is there anything in your life that makes this unacceptable? Is there something in your life that makes your Christian pilgrimage a series of stumbles and falls and failures? It is a weight, and God's call from Hebrews is to lay it aside. The race in which we are engaged is real, and great issues are at stake—ultimate loss and ultimate gain.

Weights that hinder can easily become sins that entangle us. No specific transgression is implied, such as a particular "besetting sin." Perhaps the sin is the unbelief that causes one to pull back from the journey, the lack of faith that makes one unwilling to endure the divinely appointed process of the race. The real emphasis, however, is neither on the weights nor "the sin which clings so closely" (v. 1). Attention is not directed toward ourselves in introspection or spiritual "pulse taking." The main thing is getting on with the race unencumbered, traveling light on the journey, looking not to ourselves but to Jesus.

## • Looking Only to Jesus

A great cloud of witnesses surrounds the pilgrim people, encouraging them to keep on running. Their presence suggests that it pays to be true to the promise and true to the captain of our salvation. Long centuries have passed since the Hebrews first read this letter from their writer-pastor, and the cloud of witnesses has grown to enormous proportions. Think of all the Christians of all the ages who, like St. Paul, "have fought the good fight, . . . finished the race," and "kept the faith" (2 Tim. 4:7). They are like magnets, drawing us on through the hardships of our race. Many of us have family and loved ones among that great crowd. I think of my grandfather and my father and my mother. Their finished journey of faith is great inspiration to me in the appointed process of my own. And so it is with you.

But it is not to them we look. It is to Jesus, "the pioneer and perfecter of our faith" (12:2). The heroes of faith may encourage us by their example and inspire us by their endurance, but they cannot strengthen us. Only Jesus can do that, so the writer points us to him, the greatest in the long line of faith heroes. He lived his whole life by faith. From the time of his baptism, through his temptation in the wilderness, and all through his public ministry, Jesus' testimony was, "My food is to do the will of him who sent me and to accomplish his work" (John 4:34).

All through his ministry with its good times and bad, through affirmation and hostility, Jesus lived by faith in his Father. He loved his Father, trusted him, and depended on him all the way through Gethsemane, the mocking trial, and his terrible death on the cross. He never let go his faith and trust. Like the great heroes before him, he endured great suffering without losing sight of the glory that was to come. And like them, he died before he saw the fulfillment of his dreams, yet he never gave up trust and hope. Then the Father raised him from the dead and exalted him in glory at the right hand of power. He takes his place, then, at the head of the great company of believers, as the captain of our salvation, and with them, witnesses to us that it pays to be true!

Jesus is therefore the pioneer and perfecter of faith for us. He is the chief leader, who has gone the way of faith before us and brought it to completion, being faithful all the way to the end. The phrase "pioneer and perfecter" (RSV) has been translated various ways. "The guide and end of our faith," "the source and goal," "princely leader and perfecter" are a few. I like the way it is put in the New English Bible: "Jesus, on whom faith depends from start to finish." He both perfectly embodies faith in his own life and leads us on in our journey of faith.

We are to endure in our race "looking to Jesus" (v. 2). The word translated "looking" is a special kind of word that means keeping our gaze directed toward Jesus, looking away to him with a continual and steady gaze. We are surrounded not only by the witnesses to faith, but by ensnaring sin. The only way to run with perseverance is to keep looking to Jesus and depending on him. We look not to ourselves or our faith, in either its weakness or its strength, but to him whose presence is the life of our faith.

We would probably agree that just about every testimony to spiritual failure includes words something like these: "I took my eyes off Jesus and turned them on people—and people let me down." I am not suggesting that we do *not* need each other. Oh, no! But the truth is, people will let us down. Worse than that, we let others down. Some have gotten their eyes on things and pleasures, or on jobs and making money, or on advancement and power. In a culture like ours with a thousand enticements to live for ourselves and "enjoy," there is only one way to endure. Keep looking to Jesus. An expressive phrase coming out of my childhood is "having an eye single to the glory of God."

The particular example of faith portrayed in Jesus is his

*endurance of the cross.* The life of faith, then, is life at the cross. We think of Paul's words: "Have this mind among yourselves which is yours in Christ Jesus, who, though he was in the form of God, did not count equality with God a thing to be grasped, but emptied himself . . . and became obedient unto death, even death on a cross" (Phil. 2:5–8). Whatever joy was before Jesus, he traded it off for the endurance of the cross. Its shame and reproach he gladly bore in faithful obedience to his Father's will.

We cannot keep looking to Jesus without seeing that his endurance led him to the cross, beyond which was the joy of exaltation and glory. But that joy "set before him" was not fulfilled before the suffering of his cross, nor was that joy present in the cross. He trusted, believed, and endured—then the Father raised him from the dead, and his joy was full. We cannot look to Jesus without seeing that his cross is our cross, too. The joy set before us is down a path in which stands the cross of our identification with Jesus in his obedience and self-surrender to the Father. The final joy awaits us. In the meantime we walk by faith and trust and hope—and we persevere because our hope is sure.

## • Conclusion

We began this chapter by saying that the imagery of a race is both good and bad. Let's close it by saying that, by itself the imagery is incomplete. We run our race surrounded by the shouting witnesses of faith. Our eyes are fixed on Jesus, the champion who has gone before us and who draws the whole community of faith forward toward the goal. He has been exalted in glory and is at the right hand of the throne of God.

However, our looking at Jesus is not a "far gaze." Christ is at the Father's throne, where our journey will end. He also strides before us as our pioneer and champion. And he is our companion on the journey, one with us in our humanity, sympathetic with us in our weaknesses, and interceding for us as our brother and our priest. Our starting point and our goal are one. When we come to the end

131

of our journey, we will find Jesus, the one who has been with us all the way along.

There is only one response for us: to "lay aside every weight, and sin which clings so closely," and to "run with perseverance the race that is set before us, looking to Jesus the pioneer and perfecter of our faith."

## ● Discussion Questions

1. We may not often think of ourselves as belonging to a community of faith that reaches all the way back to Abel. How might such a view influence our attitudes and behaviors as Christians? How can our oneness with our faith heritage be preserved and made a viable part of our Christian understanding? Do you think this is important?

2. Discuss the idea that God works with us in freedom and so must work through our choices, good and bad, in the accomplishment of his purposes. In your own words suggest how you think God is working out his will in human history today.

3. Some have seen the Christian life as a giant relay race. How would you interpret or illustrate this idea? Is the race imagery a good one for you? What about it is helpful or not helpful to you?

4. I have suggested that the process of running the race is as much a part of the whole picture as the goal is. Discuss this idea. If we really believed it, how would it change our understanding of what the Christian life is all about?

5. When you read that we are to "lay aside every weight, and sin which clings so closely," what things come to mind?

6. In your own words define "looking to Jesus" as we run our race. How can we do that and take care of all the legitimate responsibilities we must meet?

7. What does it mean to get your eyes off everyone and everything else and get them on Jesus? Can you illustrate from your own experience such a situation?

8. How can it be that Jesus is the one to whom we look on the journey and at the same time the one who is with us on the journey and the one we will meet at the end of the journey?

# CHAPTER · 12

# Hard Times and Holy People

Consider him who endured from sinners such hostility against himself, so that you may not grow weary or fainthearted. In your struggle against sin you have not yet resisted to the point of shedding your blood. And have you forgotten the exhortation which addresses you as sons?—

"My Son, do not regard lightly the discipline of the Lord,
nor lose courage when you are punished by him.
For the Lord disciplines him whom he loves,
and chastises every son whom he receives" [Prov. 3:11–12].

It is for discipline that you have to endure. God is treating you as sons; for what son is there whom his father does not discipline? If you are left without discipline, in which all have participated, then you are illegitimate children and not sons. Beside this, we have had earthly fathers to discipline us and we respected them. Shall we not much more be subject to the Father of spirits and live? For they disciplined us for a short time at their pleasure, but he disciplines us for our good, that we may share his holiness. For the moment all discipline seems painful rather than pleasant; later it yields the peaceful fruit of righteousness to those who have been trained by it (Heb. 12:3–11).

● Everyone knows about troubles. But not everyone knows that God is involved in our troubles and has a specific concern and intention in our endurance of them. The faint-hearted Hebrews needed to know that. They had endured hard times in the past. They knew about persecution and loss and shame. Though none had been called upon to die for their faith, martyrdom was a real and ever-present threat. But they were not to grow discouraged, because through their suffering a divine "hidden agenda" was being achieved.

I like the term "hidden agenda" in this context because it refers to God's unseen program of matters to be dealt with in people's lives. The Hebrews' suffering was not just suffering; it was also the discipline of their heavenly Father through which they would share his holiness. Since he was dealing with them as children, they were not to "regard lightly the discipline of the Lord, nor lose courage" in the process (12:5).

I wish we knew how to distinguish clearly between trials, troubles, suffering, chastening, and discipline. The writer makes no attempt to explain any of them—for that matter, neither did he explain the weights and sins we are to "lay aside" (12:1). It may be just as well, for that leaves us to search and think about the meaning of our troubles and how they relate to the purposes of God in our lives. That process could be part of the Father's discipline for us. It was not the concern of the writer to discuss the problem of human suffering. He was a pastor writing to discouraged and suffering Christian brothers and sisters, pointing them to the reality of God and his purposes in their troubles. He did it by relating their suffering to God's discipline.

## • Adversity as Discipline

I understand "discipline" in this context to mean the instructive, guiding, rebuking, chastening activity of God in our lives by which we may be brought to mature, holy character. I think it includes both specific discipline on specific occasions and the long, continuous oversight and guidance of God under which we live as Christians. A father may discipline his son for a particular transgression, but the son also lives under his father's discipline in terms of training, tutoring, and educating until he reaches majority.

There are several aspects of adversity and suffering that relate to divine discipline. In Hebrews 11, honor is given to the heroes of faith who saw the vision, embraced the promise, and made their confession. They accepted the hardships and endured the sufferings as "included in the price" of saying yes to God. Their adversities were accepted under the discipling hand of God—and they came out looking like saints!

Think of Abraham's stress as he journeyed in a strange land. The clear promise of God for a son was delayed year after year; when it was finally fulfilled, Abraham endured the agony of obedience to the word, "Take your son, your only son Isaac, whom you love, and go to the land of Moriah, and offer him there as a burnt offering" (Gen. 22:2). The discipline of the years did something to this man. He was called "the friend of God."

What about Moses and the stress of living in a strange culture, struggling between two worlds? Desperate actions drove him to the desert, but the voice of Yahweh drove him back to Egypt and his awesome encounters with the Pharaoh. Think of the years of tension, hardship, and frustration involved in the Exodus, the trek to Sinai, and the wilderness wanderings. The discipline of the years was doing something to this incredible man. He is the one through whom God created his covenant nation.

We could speak of other heroes of faith who "suffered mockings and scourgings, and even chains and imprisonment." What shall we say of these despised wanderers, "destitute, afflicted, ill-treated" (11:37)? The world's nobodies are on God's honor roll forever. Their hardships were the discipline that made them men and women of whom God said, "[I am] not ashamed to be called their God" (11:16).

Jesus himself is the greatest example of one who obeyed the Father and paid the price in hardship, adversity, and suffering. The pioneer of our salvation was made "perfect through suffering" (2:10). He endured the force of temptation (2:18; 4:15). "He learned obedience through what he suffered" (5:8) and "endured from sinners such hostility against himself (12:3). The discipline of the years did something in the life of our incarnate Lord that could not have taken place any other way. It enabled him to be our great high priest, who lived and died for us and who now lives and intercedes for us.

Everyone can see that years of facing difficulties, overcoming problems, and meeting challenges do something wonderful to the character of people who meet them and accept them in a healthy way. People who have suffered have a quality of richness in their personalities unknown to those whose lives are spared great pain. Experience and hardship and suffering are disciplines through which real character grows.

But this is not the whole biblical perspective, and we see the difference clearly in the book of Hebrews. The hardships and adversity suffered by the heroes of faith were the direct result of their commitment to their vision of God and his purposes. These hardships came because the Hebrews' obedience put them at odds with the values and practices of their culture. Their suffering was not viewed as a general kind of suffering that comes merely from being fallen humans. It was understood as the discipline of God. It was discipline in the sense that the hardships they met because of their obedience to God were also the means of making them his holy people.

The Hebrew Christians, then, were not to be discouraged in their time of adversity, because God was doing in them the very thing he had done in the saints who lived and suffered before them. As God's children they were experiencing his discipline that they might share his holiness.

## ● The Painfulness of Paying Attention

Hebrews reflects a more internal and subjective way that pain and discipline go together. Both are involved when we listen to the word of God and submit to the piercing of his two-edged sword as it divides "soul and spirit" and discerns "the thoughts and intentions of the heart" (4:12). By that word we are "laid bare to the eyes of him with whom we have to do" (4:13).

If we are continuing in earnest dialogue with our Covenant

Partner, we are put at odds with the false values of the world around us. We are also put at odds with the false values of the world within us! It is a serious and painful thing to listen to the piercing word of God. We have talked about the profound cleansing of the heart and conscience that comes through the blood of the new covenant. But as much as the Hebrews ever did, we deal with the drag of time and trouble. We have our tendencies to doubt, to be molded in subtle ways by the pressures of our self-centered and sensual society, and to drift into former ways of thinking and living.

There is pain in attentive listening to the disciplining word of God. We are warned in Hebrews not to drift or to neglect the saving word of the gospel (2:1–3). We are exhorted to look at Jesus and not lose our confidence or hope (3:1–6). We must not let unbelief or disobedience harden our hearts (3:7–4:1). We are to come near to the throne of grace (4:16; 10:22).

Are we dull of hearing (5:11)? Are we laying again and again the primary foundations, or are we really going on to maturity (6:1)? Can it be that we are getting sluggish and could fail to follow in the train of those who "through faith and patience inherit the promises" (6:12)? What if we don't "hold fast our confession" and thereby neglect our mutual responsibilities to be present in the fellowship and to encourage each other (10:23–25)? What are we going to do with the injunction to lay aside everything that hinders our progress and run with endurance our Christian race (12:1–2)? Do the dreadful words of the potential for apostasy have any serious meaning for us (6:4–8; 10:26–31)?

There is neither suffering nor discipline in these exhortations and warnings if all we do is read, define, and explain them. There is pain, discipline, and sometimes punishment in them if we are in attentive and obedient conversation with the One who speaks to us! They expose our apathy and dullness of hearing. (One of my grandfather's prayers was, "O Lord, help us to get the ear wax out of our ears, so we can hear what you have to say!")

The word of God lays bare our unbelief and the subtle coolness and aloofness of our hearts. It discloses the weights that hinder our journey, and it demands our radical response. That response can be nothing other than the pain of repentance and confession and surrender to the judgment and healing of God. It can mean nothing other than the joy of humble acceptance of his forgiveness and cleansing; nothing other than renewed obedience to his will. In short, it means accepting God's discipline.

If we take this attitude toward the word of God, then the suffering we experience as the result of our own failures and blunders can also be accepted as part of the disciplining process that ultimately works for our growth in holiness. We have all acted in unworthy ways, have made poor choices, and have manifested un-Christlike attitudes. And we suffer. We know the pain of failure and the anguish of guilt. We hurt when we disappoint or injure another. We love and care but don't know how to do the right thing or what to say to make it right. We want to raise our children well—and find out later how poorly we did. We want to be a good husband or wife or son or daughter but the things we say or do are not received in the way we hoped. And we suffer.

What shall we say of these feelings? If we open them to God and expose them to his word, the sufferings that follow from our own faults become the very means by which we are disciplined by the Father for growth in wisdom and holy character.


## ● Pain Without Discipline

But what about the general suffering of Christians that comes from our being a part of the fallen world of mankind? Some people say that for Christians, all suffering is only rightly understood as the Father's discipline, correction, and direction. I cannot accept that with regard to "all suffering." I believe suffering can have a sanctifying, maturing effect on us if we are enabled by it to discern some destructive self-centeredness or a lack of prayer-fulness or an unworthy motive or attitude. In that case we can accept our suffering as part of the discipline of God and through it be led to confess and deal with the changes we perceive God wants to bring about in us.

But much of the suffering of God's people in our world hurts too much to count for anything in enrichment of mind and spirit. I am thinking of innocent victims of earthquake, fire, flood, and famine. I am reminded of Christians who have been the casualties of crime and war, violence and terrorism. And I remember those who have fallen prey to drunken drivers, random diseases, birth injuries, or physical abuse. The listing has no end.

To say that these kinds of sufferings are the punishment or discipline of God for our holiness is both true and false. I find it impossible to think that God would let us be paralyzed so that we would walk closer to him. Or, for me personally, that God would permit our firstborn to be a brain-damaged child so that her mother and I would submit to the discipline of God and thus be brought to maturity and the development of compassionate and holy character. I cannot believe that for the Christian all suffering is only rightly understood as the Father's discipline.

However, there is a sense in which the statement is profoundly true. Suffering and adversity of all kinds becomes discipline for God's people when we see them not as events in themselves, but as situations under the sovereignty of God. He is present in all that we experience, actively working out his "hidden agenda"—our sharing his holiness. His discipline becomes effective when we can say yes to both the suffering experience and God's purpose for us in it.

## • Acceptance and Response

There is still another dimension of God's discipline in our suffering and adversity. What is it that makes a particular discipline effective? What must be present for an exhortation to really exhort? Under what conditions does a warning actually succeed in warning?

We would probably agree that among the general population,

perhaps among Christians, the experience of tragedy as often drives one away from God as toward him. Adversity may be seen by one person as a divine vindictive punishment, by another as the result of bad personal choices, by still another as fate or just bad luck. There are others who will view their adversities, however bad, as situations under God that are being used by him as a means of discipline toward holiness. The difference is not in the intention of God, nor in the character of the experience of suffering, but in the discernment and the response of the sufferer.

Perhaps that is why the passage from Proverbs quoted in Hebrews 12:5 is so important to the writer: "My son, do not regard lightly the discipline of the Lord, nor lose courage when you are punished by him." The intention of God is that "he disciplines us for our good, that we may share his holiness. . . . it yields the peaceful fruit of righteousness to those who have been trained by it" (12:10–11).

But what if discipline is lightly regarded or rejected or despised? Suffering, then, is just suffering, heartache is just heartache, tragedy is just tragedy, and we are left to ourselves to cry or rage or fight or escape. If the idea of some pervasive, overriding concern of God for us in our sufferings is rejected, how can anything good or healing or holy ever come out of our troubles? If, however, we lose heart and courage and give up in our sufferings, the disciplining, sanctifying purposes of God are as effectively thwarted as if we had rejected them. A literal translation of 12:5 is "You have forgotten altogether the exhortation which dialogues with you as sons." If we refuse discipline, we refuse the dialogue and break the relationship. If we accept it, endure it, and keep the conversation alive, the relationship is made even more strong and intimate.

That is why the author takes such pains to make the point that God is not absent when we suffer. When in suffering we feel chastened or disciplined, it is not a sign that God is distant or angry or vindictive. Yet the discipline we experience is not a sign of divine approval or pleasure; it is a sign of *divine relationship*. God is present as our Father and is "toward us" as his children, not "out there" and not "over against" us. He is present and in continuing dialogue with us through all the mysteries of our lives, seeking to work his hidden agenda for our holiness. Earthly fathers discipline on the basis of what seems good to *them*—in spite of the old line, "This hurts me more than it hurts you!" We have the assurance that our heavenly Father's discipline is based on what is really good for *us*. In the relationship we are the beneficiaries.

### • Conclusion

We have noted that the author of Hebrews does not deal with the general subject of human sufferings, nor does he ever say just what the sufferings of the Hebrews were, nor how we are to recognize the discipline of God when we are receiving it. I think his reason for this is partly that definitions would only lead to more definitions and explanations would only be multiplied by more words of explanation. Such activities seem to be the special gift of Bible teachers, commentators, and preachers. But mostly, I think, the writer is not mainly concerned with suffering or with discipline—either is only a means to an end. His real concern is with sharing the holiness of God, the practical result of which is "the peaceful fruit of righteousness" (12:11).

The writer exhorts, "Don't despise what God is wanting to do. Don't give up on what God is wanting to do. He is really present in our sufferings, and what he wants to do is to make us his holy people." Our Father's discipline works for our holiness as we, amid suffering, open ourselves to him to let him deal with our motives, values, and ego. God's hidden agenda is accomplished when our sufferings and trials, our weights and sins, our whole selves are brought to the cross and surrendered there to Jesus, our priest, who "suffered outside the gate in order to sanctify the people with his own blood" (13:12).

But the author of Hebrews never lets us get far from our active participation in the pilgrim journey as the people of God. The cleansing of our sin and defilement, our separation to God in holiness, is not a restful "state of being" as much as a dynamic and personal relationship in the context of a journey.

In the body of believers, then, we are to lift up each other's hands, strengthen each other's knees, encourage each other's hearts, and move on ahead. In relation to others we are to be "instruments of peace." In relation to God the command is to strive "for the holiness without which no man will see the Lord" (12:14), that is, conformity to and participation in his holiness. It involves the cleansing of the heart and conscience and the purity of character "which has been set apart for God and consecrated by his hallowing spirit" (Hugh Montefiore).

Striving for such holiness cleanses the eyes of the soul for the vision of God and cleanses the heart and life for the time when "we shall be like him, for we shall see him as he is" (1 John 3:2).

## • Discussion Questions

1. Why are people inclined to think that their trouble and suffering mean that God does not exist or, if he does, he does not care or is angry or vindictive?

2. How do you respond to the general definition I have given for discipline, namely, "the instructive, guiding, rebuking, chastening activity of God in our lives by which we may be brought to mature, holy character"? What other illustrations can you suggest besides the father-son relationship?

3. The heroes of faith took God's way and accepted the consequences, good and bad, including adversity and suffering. In what sense can we say that these hardships, experienced because of obedience, were discipline?

4. What is the difference between the general discipline of life that builds character, such as the hard life of a homestead farmer who faces adversity and hardship and endures, and the discipline of God in the farmer's life?

5. Discuss the idea that God's discipline comes through the rebukes, the exposure, the warnings, and the exhortations of his Word? How does that produce suffering? Does discipline always involve some adverse element such as hardship or suffering?

6. "I got too busy and didn't take time for myself or my family or my church, so God laid me out on this hospital bed so I would have nowhere to look but up to him." What is true about that statement? What is false about it?

7. How do you respond to the idea that rejected discipline, or discipline that produces discouragement and loss of hope, breaks relationship? Can you illustrate how discipline truly accepted increases intimacy and strength of the relationship?

8. What examples from your life illustrate when God's discipline was recognized and accepted and led you to a more mature walk with him?

# CHAPTER · 13

# Yesterday, Today, and Forever

Remember your leaders, those who spoke to you the word of God; consider the outcome of their life, and imitate their faith. Jesus Christ is the same yesterday and today and for ever. Do not be led away by diverse and strange teachings; for it is well that the heart be strengthened by grace, not by foods; which have not benefited their adherents. We have an altar from which those who serve the tent have no right to eat. For the bodies of those animals whose blood is brought into the sanctuary by the high priest as a sacrifice for sin are burned outside the camp. So Jesus also suffered outside the gate in order to sanctify the people through his own blood. Therefore let us go forth to him outside the camp, and bear the abuse he endured (Heb. 13:7–13).

● As we have seen, Hebrews was written to awaken, to encourage, to exhort, to warn, and especially to declare to its readers how completely God has met their needs in Jesus Christ. Through the new covenant inaugurated by his death as their great high priest, they have been granted priceless privileges. The purpose of the epistle, in Floyd Filson's words, is to "sweep aside any doubts concerning the truth and crucial importance of the gospel, and to make clear the completeness and adequacy of God's work in Christ." The acceptance or indifference of the Hebrews was of utmost importance; their decision was crucial because it would determine their spiritual status, then and for all time.

The passage under examination in this chapter of our study contains "one of the greatest single sentences in the New

Testament" about Christ, the final and supreme revelation of God to men, according to T. H. Robinson. The reality of its truth, Robinson says, "gives the human soul its certainty, the church its continuity."

Let me translate the verse as literally as I can: "Jesus Christ, yesterday and today the same—and unto the ages" (v. 8). It is a sort of magnet verse by which we may go back through Hebrews and pull together some of the great teachings about Christ and about our Christian faith and pilgrimage.

At first reading, the verse seems to stand alone, unrelated to the verses that surround it. Let's look at the context and try to discover some inner connection.

The Hebrews are called to "remember your leaders, those who spoke to you the word of God; consider the outcome of their life, and imitate their faith" (13:7). It could be that these leaders were among those who had heard the word "declared by the Lord" and had "attested" it (2:3) at the time of the founding of the church. These apostolic missionaries were examples not only in their preaching, but in the quality of their faith—faith that endured through a triumphant death. Though they were now gone, their death in the faith was an inspiration, and the Hebrews were exhorted to take a careful look, that is, "consider the outcome of their life" (v. 7).

"Remember your leaders, imitate their faith!" It is good to remember. I think of some of the people who have been "leaders" in my life, from whom I have heard the word and in whom I have seen the Lord. Their remembrance is a powerful force in my life toward faith and loyalty and godliness. Some are now in heaven; I have been privileged to see "the outcome of their life," and as I consider it, I am inspired to "imitate their faith" (v. 7). The word to the Hebrews was not to imitate their leaders, but to imitate their faith—their faith in Jesus Christ, its pioneer and perfecter (12:2).

This exhortation in verse 7 leads naturally to the grand declaration of verse 8, "Jesus Christ, yesterday and today the same—and unto the ages." The Hebrews' leaders were gone, but

Jesus remains. Over and over again in Hebrews we have been reminded of the transient character of life, for us and for those who through centuries have been God's instruments and spokesmen. Of all the heroes of the faith chapter it is said, "These all died in faith" (11:13), and the "former priests were many in number, because they were prevented by death from continuing in office" (7:23). The old saints were gone, the leaders of the Hebrews were gone, and now both the Hebrews and their concerned pastor-writer are gone. "These all died in faith."

I pray it may be said of us that we died in faith—it will surely be said that we died. Is the cycle never broken? Has anyone, will anyone, ever come into our world who is qualitatively different, in fact permanent? "Jesus Christ, yesterday and today the same—and unto the ages!"

## • The Reference Point

Verse 9 draws a contrast between the changeless Christ, who first declared the "great salvation," and the "diverse and strange teachings" that were going around. The emphasis on remembering their departed leaders and imitating their faith may indicate that the Hebrews were turning away from the word that had been spoken to them and were getting involved in destructive teachings and ceremonial meals.

The good word for them was that what is good for the heart is grace, not the ritual foods of foreign doctrines. Grace comes from the altar of the cross, on which our priest became the willing sacrifice that redeems us from all demonic power now and forever. Jesus said that his flesh was food indeed, and his blood was drink indeed—but his words were spirit and life (John 6:55, 63). Those who turned back from the life offered at the altar of grace to serve the "tent" of the old covenant and old rituals could not also share in Jesus, the "bread of life." Their apostle and high priest was not absent from them, but present in their worship as the spoken word of God.

Jesus is present in ours also. Our recognition of his constancy as the pioneer and perfecter of our faith will save us from false ideas and practices that can fragment and destroy the fellowship. So verse 8 has a context: Look to your leaders, but look to your supreme leader who is the same 'Yesterday and today and forever."

Usually this verse is interpreted to mean that Christ is the eternal, changeless Son of God. From eternity to eternity he is the same. An old commentator put it this way: Christ is exalted above all change in fortune and in feeling; above all vicissitudes he is the unchanging and abiding head of the church; the same, yesterday, today, and forever. It is good for us to pause and think about such things. Is there anything in this old world that does not change? Birth, growth, development, maturity, decay, death, and new life—all these terms are transition terms that speak of inevitable change. At the same time, our hearts cry out for permanence. The words of Henry Lyte's hymn express a universal longing:

> Change and decay in all around I see;
> O Thou who changest not, abide with me!

Jesus is that one who does not change. Times do, cultures and civilizations do. So do the ways we think. What can keep our understanding of God anywhere near on track through the passing centuries and changing philosophies and world views? Only this one thing: A constant reality persists through all time and transition. There is one changeless, immutable element—no, not an element—a person. It is Christ, whose unchanging character makes possible all true thinking about God. Man's conceptions "may change, and as one age succeeds another the stress may be varied and the angle of vision moved, but the great reality is changeless, invariable, immovable" (T. H. Robinson).

Whatever world view we hold, whatever influence new science and technology may have on the way we look at our physical world, there is Jesus. He is the ultimate point of reference for our understanding of the world, ourselves, and our God, precisely because he does not change. The writer to the Hebrews realized that the words of the psalmist were words about the unchanging Christ:

> Of old thou didst lay the foundation of the earth,
>   and the heavens are the work of thy hands.
> They will perish, but thou dost endure;
>   they will all wear out like a garment.
> Thou changest them like raiment, and they pass away;
>   but thou art the same, and thy years have no end.
> The children of thy servants shall dwell secure;
>   their posterity shall be established before thee."
>               (Ps. 102:25–28, quoted in part in Heb. 1:10–12)

Andrew Murray wrote some "timeless" words on this theme about a hundred years ago: "All that he was yesterday, he is today. All that he was yesterday in the past of the great eternity, as the object of the Father's delight and the bearer and dispenser of the Father's life and love, he is today. All that he was on earth, with his meek and gentle and sympathizing heart, he is today. All that he has been on his throne, in sending down his spirit, in working mighty things in and on behalf of his church, in revealing himself in joy unspeakable to trusting souls, he is today. All that he is he can be to you today. *And the only reason that you ever had to look back to a yesterday that was better than today, was that you did not know, or failed to trust this Jesus, who was waiting to make each today a new revelation and a larger experience of the grace of yesterday*" (from *The Holiest of All*). "Jesus Christ, the same yesterday and today—and unto the ages."

## • Just Yesterday

There is, however, another way of looking at this verse which, it seems to me, ties it even more closely to the theme of Hebrews and especially to the context of chapter 13.

The meaning is not primarily the timelessness and the eternal changelessness of Christ, though these are profound truths. I believe the best way to understand the verse is to interpret the word "yesterday" the way it is used in the rest of the Bible (oddly enough, only eight times in all). It means literally the day before today (1 Sam. 20:27; 2 Sam. 15:20; 2 Kings 9:26; John 4:52; Acts 7:28, where Stephen refers to Moses, Exod. 2:11–14). Job's friend Bildad says, "We are but of yesterday and know nothing, for our days on earth are a shadow" (Job 8:9). The other place the word is used is Psalms 90:4, "For a thousand years in thy sight are but as yesterday when it is past, or as a watch in the night." "Yesterday," then, instead of meaning "from all eternity past," denotes "just a little while ago," or a brief time past.

Let's look at the verse in Hebrews from this point of view. The Hebrews were part of a congregation of second-generation Christians who probably heard the word from those who heard the Lord. The message of their pastor to them was that just yesterday, just a little while ago, Jesus became what he is now—and what he will be for all ages. Something happened yesterday. A profound and everlasting change took place in the changeless Son of God. Just yesterday the sovereign, eternal God did something in Christ that will never be undone for all eternity—that something is *incarnation.*

Can we really grasp what happened yesterday? For us it was many yesterdays ago, but in the long view, not so many. The eternal Son of God laid aside the splendor of his Father's presence and entered into our human situation, taking to himself fully and utterly our humanity. God became a real man in Jesus, yesterday. He was "made lower than the angels" (2:9). The pioneer of our salvation, the Son of God, "learned obedience through what he suffered," was in fact "made perfect through suffering" (2:11; 5:8). Since we are flesh and blood, "he himself partook of the same nature . . . made like his brethren in every respect" (2:14, 17). He "has suffered, and been tempted . . . in every respect" (2:18; 4:15). The Lord of glory "offered up prayers and supplications, with loud cries and tears" to God (5:7), and endured great "hostility against himself" (12:3). That's what happened yesterday—incarnation.

And do we know that yesterday he died for us? The one through whom God spoke his saving word "made purification for sins"

(1:3). He was made lower than the angels "because of the suffering of death" (2:9). He himself partook of our same nature that "through death he might destroy him who has the power of death, that is, the devil" (2:14). He was made like us in order to "make expiation for the sins of the people" (2:17), and he "put away sin by the sacrifice of himself" (9:26). "We have been sanctified through the offering of the body of Jesus Christ once for all" (10:10). Our sovereign Lord Jesus "endured the cross . . . suffered outside the gate in order to sanctify the people through his own blood" (12:2; 13:12). That's what happened yesterday—crucifixion, our sacrifice for sin.

And can we ever grasp the wondrous truth that yesterday his Father raised him from the dead and exalted him in glory? We do not see the final triumph, but "we see Jesus, . . . crowned with glory and honor" (2:9). "It was fitting that we should have such a high priest, holy, blameless, unstained, separated from sinners, exalted above the heavens" (7:26). He has entered into the Holy Place, taking "his own blood" (9:12). He has entered "into heaven itself" (9:24). He is seated with power and authority at "the right hand of God" (10:12; 12:2). Do we understand what happened just yesterday? The great God of peace "brought again from the dead our Lord Jesus, the great shepherd of the sheep" (13:20). That's what happened yesterday—resurrection.

God takes time seriously. He takes our time and our times and our whole human existence seriously. And yesterday God broke into the stream of our human history, coming fully into our world, going all the way to the cross and the grave, from which he arose on the third day and was exalted in power. That was yesterday.

## • Still Today

But it is not yesterday; it is today. Yesterday was incarnation, yesterday was crucifixion, yesterday was resurrection. But what about today? Here, I believe, is the crucial point of our text. Jesus, "the same yesterday," does not only mean his changelessness from eternity. It means that just yesterday he did, in fact, change—profoundly and forever. Yesterday was the awesome change in the very godhead when Jesus became incarnate, when he died once for all for our sins and when he rose again to the right hand of the Father. That change is real and permanent and effectual in our lives. It can never be unmade, changed back, or rescinded.

It has been emphasized in these Bible studies that the incarnation of Jesus is forever. His entrance into our humanity was not a temporary experience but a permanent involvement. Jesus not only came all the way into our humanity, but he came for all time. In his ascension he apparently did not take his human body, but he did take with him our full human nature, back into the very heart of God. Our high priest, at the right hand of the Father, is just as human today—this today—as he became yesterday. He is our brother now. The precious gift I would pray for you is that right now where you are, you would see Jesus totally, fully, completely human. He is our brother now. Today.

Jesus is the one who delivers us from our fear of death (2:15) and deals with our sins with mercy and faithfulness toward us (2:17). He is our tempted brother who knows how bad temptations can be and with great empathy invites us, in our temptations, to come to the "throne of grace, that we may receive mercy and find grace to help in time of need" (4:16). He doesn't save us from "outside," but like us he learned obedience through what he suffered. He becomes, then, "the source of eternal salvation to all who obey him" (5:9).

Because Jesus lives and intercedes for us, the salvation he gives us continues to the uttermost, for all our needs "for all time" (7:25). The same idea is expressed in the imagery of the new covenant. God's promise through Christ continues to be effective because it is "mediated" continually by our living priest. It is not a promise simply remembered and recorded; it is kept constantly real by the mediation of Jesus (8:6; 12:24).

Can our deepest hearts be really cleansed from sin, or are we after all just dealing with nice religious ideas? What our Lord became yesterday, our sacrifice for sin, he still is today. He can truly "purify" our "conscience from dead works to serve the living God." We may "draw near with a true heart in full assurance of faith, with our hearts sprinkled clean from an evil conscience and our bodies washed with pure water" (9:11–14; 10:19–22).

And what of today? He is now our brother. His blood still atones for sin; his intercession is still effectual. He has opened the way to God and still bids us welcome.

## ● Even Tomorrow

But what of tomorrow? "Jesus Christ, yesterday and today the same—and unto the ages!" The word "ages"—also translated "aeons"—was used in at least two ways in the first century. It was used to mean "forever." Jesus used it that way when he gave the Great Commission of Matthew 28:20: "And lo, I am with you always, to the close of the age."

In some religious groups (such as the gnostics), however, "ages," or "aeons," were not thought of in terms of time, but of power, such as cosmic forces or gods that exercised control over their lives. People lived in fear of these supposed powers and sought to appease them through secret worship ceremonies and rituals. I suppose some contemporary examples of such beliefs would be astrology or metaphysical or religious science kinds of doctrines, or perhaps Eastern religions that seek to find fulfillment through harmony with the elemental spirits or the rhythms or the spiritual vibrations or the inner light of the universe.

The freedom from fear and the confidence we gain from the gospel is that the Christ who has become what he is will *always* be what he is. There is no returning for him to the hidden and secure realms of his heavenly home while we struggle against unseen powerful forces to achieve our salvation. In his incarnation, death, and resurrection he has come to the depth of where we are, has won for us the victory, and is now our pioneer on the journey, all the way. Paul would say that "neither death, nor life, nor angels, nor principalities, nor things present, nor things to come, nor powers, nor height, nor depth, nor anything else in all creation, will be able to separate us from the love of God in Christ Jesus our Lord" (Rom. 8:38–39).

What, then, of tomorrow? What of our insecurities, hopes, and unfulfilled dreams? What is to become of our goals and desires? Tomorrow is a very big word for us—big for us as persons and as the people of God.

There are those who believe profoundly—and I am one of them—that we are beginning to see the end of civilization as we have known it. Our future as a democratic society is far from secure, and the future of Christianty is tenuous. Evangelicalism in the Western world is fragmented and often moves in self-destructive directions. Our pluralism, our lack of cohesive vision, and our confused understanding of our task could continue to lessen the hold of the Christian faith in our world.

These views are open to discussion, but the point is, tomorrow is crucial for us and for the Church of Jesus Christ. We have not yet become what we must become to be effective as the people of God. But there is tomorrow! What Jesus Christ became yesterday, he is still today—and unto the ages. No new thing is ever needed. Once for all he died, once for all he accomplished the sacrifice, once for all he revealed the Father—and he will be all we ever need for all the tomorrows of our journey. He will forever be what he became—yesterday.

The writer to the Hebrews would send us on our journey as he sent his first readers: "I appeal to you, brethren, bear with my word of exhortation" (13:22). He would have us carry in our hearts, as we go, the words of benediction: "Now may the God of peace who brought again from the dead our Lord Jesus, the great shepherd of the sheep, by the blood of the eternal covenant, equip you in everything good that you may do his will, working in you that which is pleasing in his sight, through Jesus Christ; to whom be glory for ever and ever. Amen" (13:20–21).

## • Discussion Questions

1. Having completed this study of Hebrews, how would you characterize the people to whom it was written? How would you summarize the writer's message to them?

2. What "leaders" do you remember, and how have they influenced your life? (The word "leader" is not a formal word like "apostle," or "elder," or "bishop." It actually means "the ones who led you.")

3. Verse 8 is usually interpreted to signify the changelessness of Christ from eternity to eternity. What does it mean to you that he is the "changeless Christ"?

4. The words quoted from Andrew Murray are a good statement to memorize. What is your response to the sentence in italics? How can we get those who need them the most to believe them?

5. I have given a different interpretation to Hebrews 13:8 than one usually given. After looking up the Biblical uses of "yesterday," summarize what you think it means and how it relates to verse 8.

6. Discuss the idea that a profound change took place in the changeless Christ "yesterday?"

7. How do you respond to the question, "And what about tomorrow?" What are some of your own hopes and dreams for tomorrow for yourself? your church fellowship? your country? other?

8. Discuss the word "ages" in terms of powers. Why do you think many people feel under some sort of control of universal forces or spirits or the heavenly bodies? Do you know Christians who feel this way in spite of what they have been taught otherwise?

9. By all means memorize Hebrews 13:20–21!